PRAISE FOR *INVESTING AHEAD*

"I have known Tom Curran for more than forty years. Not only is he successful, he is a proponent of advising folks in easy-to-understand language. Mr. Curran does a marvelous job pointing out the journey one takes when securing their financial security. He recounts personal experience and thoughtfully illustrates with clear anecdotes to show that choices made early in life may rob us of our future security. His writing is fluid using points and rules throughout. This should be a 'must-read' for persons who want to be in charge of their investments."

—**Peter E. Bulger,** *adjunct professor of finance, former securities regulator, and executive associated with several investment firms*

"Being a serial entrepreneur and investor in hundreds of young companies over the past forty years, I have been dedicated to the mission of 'Economic Freedom for Everyone.' Over the same period of time, from the world of finance, Tom Curran has been dedicated to the same mission. Through this book, he provides an actionable prospective to a far greater audience than either of us are able to reach individually. If everyone read this book and internalized the fundamental concepts, their quality of life would be substantially improved."

—**Michael D. Marvin,** *chairman emeritus, MapInfo; chairman, American University in Bulgaria; board member of other young companies and not-for-profits; and a client of Tom Curran for thirty-five years*

"I am a retired physician. During the nearly forty years that I have been a Curran client, Tom has taught me the stock market investing methodology and discipline necessary for me to become well off financially, be in a position to help my family, and be able to enjoy a secure retirement. Tom's new book, *Investing Ahead: Eight Essentials for Achieving Financial Security*, is an eminently readable, practical, and useful guide. It recalls the many conversations that I have had with Tom over the years and includes some insightful ways of thinking about savings and spending—about the future value of money, as Tom puts it. *Investing Ahead* reflects Tom's good character and rare investment expertise, attributes which underpin a terrific read."

—Jim Schnur, MD, *former assistant professor of radiology, Harvard Medical School; staff radiologist, Banner-University Medical Center; and a client of Tom Curran for thirty-nine years*

"Tom Curran has been my financial advisor for the last thirty years. Many colleagues of mine have retained and released five or six financial advisors over the same time frame. I have never felt compelled to make a change for the simple reason that I have done well with Tom's advice. I commend Tom for writing this book so that he can share with a larger audience his knowledge and they may appreciate his straightforward method to creating wealth. Tom's approach is not a get-rich-quick scheme. Rather, it provides straightforward guiding principles that are easily understood. A common response from my professional friends and colleagues when we discuss finances is that financial concepts are complicated, difficult to understand, and are best left to their financial advisors or accountants. The approaches outlined in Tom's book are easily understood and can be implemented with minimal effort in partnership with one's own financial advisor or on their own. This book is a must-read for individuals starting out in their careers. If they follow Tom's advice, they will be assured a retirement without financial concerns."

—Aubrey M. Palestrant, MD, *FSIR, fellow, American Heart Institute; client of Tom Curran for thirty years*

INVESTING AHEAD

INVESTING AHEAD

EIGHT ESSENTIALS FOR ACHIEVING FINANCIAL SECURITY

THOMAS J. CURRAN

Advantage®

Published by Advantage, Charleston, South Carolina.
Member of Advantage Media Group.

ADVANTAGE is a registered trademark, and the Advantage colophon is a trademark of Advantage Media Group, Inc.

Printed in the United States of America.

10 9 8 7 6 5 4 3 2 1

ISBN: 978-1-64225-109-8
LCCN: 2021924930

Cover design by David Taylor.
Layout design by Mary Hamilton.

This publication is designed to provide accurate and authoritative information in regard to the subject matter covered. It is sold with the understanding that the publisher is not engaged in rendering legal, accounting, or other professional services. If legal advice or other expert assistance is required, the services of a competent professional person should be sought.

Advantage Media Group is proud to be a part of the Tree Neutral® program. Tree Neutral offsets the number of trees consumed in the production and printing of this book by taking proactive steps such as planting trees in direct proportion to the number of trees used to print books. To learn more about Tree Neutral, please visit **www.treeneutral.com**.

Advantage Media Group is a publisher of business, self-improvement, and professional development books and online learning. We help entrepreneurs, business leaders, and professionals share their Stories, Passion, and Knowledge to help others Learn & Grow. Do you have a manuscript or book idea that you would like us to consider for publishing? Please visit **advantagefamily.com**.

To my wife, Peg. I cherish the fact that we met for the first time in elementary school and began dating as sophomores in high school. You have been a big part of all I have done. More accurately, you and I did it all together. Without you, there would be no book.

CONTENTS

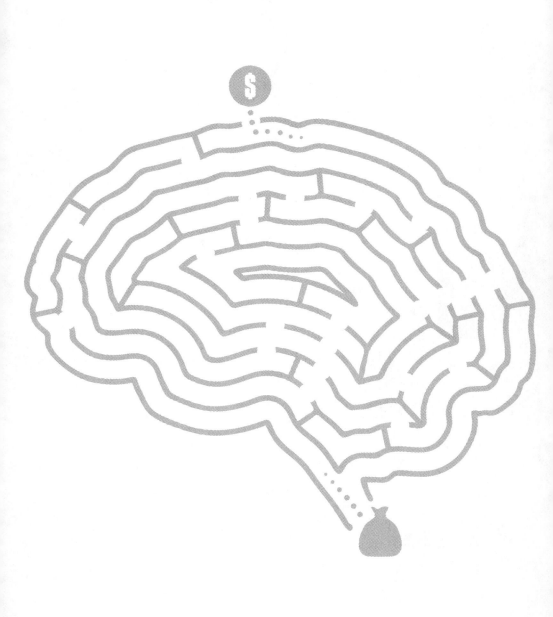

ABOUT THE AUTHOR

Anyone can make money. Only a few can acquire wealth. Tom Curran knows how. And he can teach you how to invest ahead.

With more than fifty years of experience in the securities business, Tom Curran has built a reputation and a track record that are synonymous with consistency. Tom still has his first client. He's still married to his high school sweetheart. And he still uses the same investment formula—the formula he will share with you in this book—that he used to acquire millions from the ground up, in good times and in bad.

His approach is not about overnight wealth. It requires only a focused outlook, one just about anyone who's serious about investing can learn if they're really committed to deferring immediate pleasure for long-term gains. Just as important, Tom is dedicated to sharing the lessons—good and not so good—he's learned as a lifetime investor. He wrote this book because he wants more investors to take a step back and think about the topics that matter most.

A member of his firm's investment committee, Tom formulates the investment strategy and follows the Global Investment Performance Standards. These voluntary guidelines are used by investment management firms throughout the world to encourage full disclosure and fair representation of investment performance.

Prior to forming his company, Tom served as managing director and certified portfolio manager of Curran Investment Management of Wachovia Securities, where he received firm-wide recognition as a Platinum member of Wachovia's Chairman's Circle of Excellence.

One of only six advisors nationwide to be named to *Research* magazine's 2006 Advisor Hall of Fame, he was recognized for his superior client service and earned the respect of his peers and the broader community for the honor he reflects on his profession.

Tom began his career at First Albany Corporation, where he was senior vice president and managing director of First Albany Asset Management. He held a number of respected positions at First Albany, including corporate syndicate manager, corporate and government bonds manager, and manager of life insurance and estate planning.

Tom grew up in the Brewerytown neighborhood of Philadelphia, before moving to Folsom, Pennsylvania, in suburban Delaware County. His parents, Thomas and Marguerite Curran, instilled in him the notion that he could achieve anything he set his mind to, and despite living in a blue-collar community, they never doubted that he would go on to attend college.

A graduate of Temple University, Tom received his MBA from the Wharton School at the University of Pennsylvania. He was a Fels Fellow at the University of Pennsylvania's Fels Institute of Local and State Government.

Tom has been married to his high-school sweetheart for over fifty-five years. Although they began their journey together with little money, they managed to raise a family and grow together. The children even contributed to many of Tom's early business ventures!

In 2005, Tom founded his own business, Curran Wealth Management, on the belief that too much advice in the financial services industry is self-serving and does not maximize benefits for clients. Achieving financial security for people is more about long-term advice. It is not about products that "sell" with commissions and charges that enrich the industry more than its clients.

Most of all, Tom Curran is an investor who wants to help other investors move forward with confidence—and invest ahead.

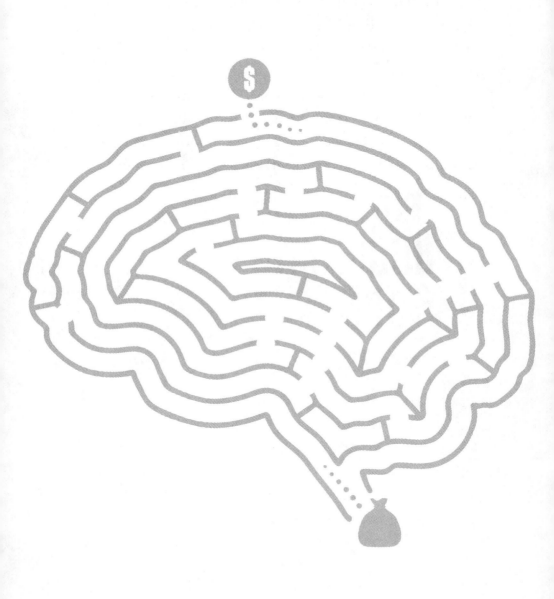

WHY I WROTE THIS BOOK, AND WHAT IT CAN DO FOR YOU

You probably picked up this book because you want to know how to become wealthy. Possibly it's because you aren't there yet, and you are interested in learning how to invest what money you do have. Maybe you simply want to hold on to your money better so that you have enough left over to invest. I know the feeling, and I can show you some ways to do that. I can show you what I did and do with my own money. Finally, I can share with you some of the advice I've been offering my clients for more than fifty years. If you follow that advice, you, too, can improve your life, achieve success, and yes, become wealthy.

IT STARTED WITH A CIGAR

I didn't get wealthy by winning the lottery (I don't play it) or inheriting from a rich uncle (I don't have one). If I had to boil down my strategy to one sentence, I would say I did it by thinking ahead. "Sure," you might say. "I can think ahead, too, and I want to be rich, the sooner, the better."

Then I might ask you about that cup of designer coffee in your hand.

And you might tell me, "It costs less than a tank of gas." Or you might even say, "I deserve it." Both of those statements are probably true, but they aren't going to get you any closer to your goal of wealth. What will get you closer to it is thinking ahead.

We didn't have designer coffee when I was young, but we did have cigars—in my case, cheap cigars. Peggy, my wife, was earning less than $5,000 a year as an elementary school teacher, and I was going to graduate school on a fellowship. Our one-bedroom apartment cost us $115 a month, about 25 percent of our earnings. I decided that thinking about what a dollar is worth right now isn't the best way to think about money. It's what that dollar will be worth in the future. I took a look at those cheap cigars of mine and did some calculations based on the historical records of inflation. Yes, I really did that. In fact, I actually invested in an HP calculator because I wanted to be able to determine the future value of money. Then I stopped buying the cigars and invested the money instead. In other words, I deferred my pleasure of the now (enjoying the cigar), knowing the money I saved would serve me better. If my son, who is my business partner, does the same thing and applies the same numbers, he could be worth more than one billion when he is my age.

That's one of the first things we'll look at in this book—changing your outlook. I'm not sure why it wasn't that difficult for me. My mother always said I was old before my time. From a young age, I always considered the consequences, and in the case of the cigars, I just saw a path that meant putting off instant gratification.

Between taxes and consumption, many people have nothing left to invest these days. It doesn't have to be that way, and in this book, I'm going to show you how to change that. We're going to look at emotional intelligence, because if spending and saving money were simply logical matters, most people would have plenty. I don't care how smart you are or how logical. When it comes to making decisions, emotion is the great neutralizer. Can you cry and think at the same time? Can you worry and think? Neither can I. Many times my clients tell me, "You seem so calm. Don't you ever get upset?" I tell them that's a luxury I cannot allow myself. Not when I'm working.

You may have heard about what's become known over the years as "the marshmallow test," conducted at Stanford University starting back in 1960 to study when the control of deferred gratification develops in children. Subjects from the ages of four to six were led into a room, empty of distractions, where a treat of their choice was placed on a table by a chair. The subjects were told they could eat that treat right then, or if they waited for fifteen minutes, they could have both this treat and a second one. In follow-up studies, researchers found unexpected correlations between the results of the marshmallow test and the success of the children many years later. The first follow-up study, in 1988, showed that preschool children who delayed gratification longer in the self-imposed delay paradigm were described more than ten years later by their parents as adolescents who were significantly more competent.[1]

I wouldn't be surprised if they were wealthier than their peers as well.

To be successful, you need emotional intelligence. Your investing strategies can't be motivated by emotional preferences like fear or greed. They must be motivated by data. I like to remind beginning investors that, in the early days of baseball, tobacco-chewing old-timers would sign players based on their gut instincts about an individual player. But today, it's all about metrics—in baseball and in the investment field. Data has all the answers. Don't let emotion distract you from that.

A young man whose inheritance I was managing wanted to know if it was all right if he bought a new truck.

"How much is it?" I asked.

"Twenty thousand," he told me. "Do you think it's worth it?"

How would you answer that question? Again, the decision requires thinking ahead.

"The question isn't whether you think the truck is worth $20,000," I told him. "The question is whether it's worth $400,000 because that could be the future value of that money."

Notice I didn't tell him whether he should or shouldn't buy the truck. That was his decision. I'm not going to lecture to you either. What I am going to do is share my knowledge and experiences with you so that you can make your own decisions.

---

1   Walter Mischel, Yuichi Shoda, and Monica L. Rodriguez. "Delay of Gratification in Children." *Science* 244, no. 4907 (1989): 933–38, October 4, 2020, http://www.jstor.org/stable/1704494.

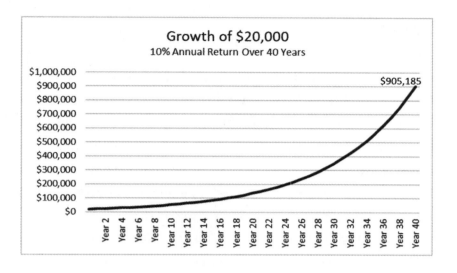

THE DREAM AND THE REALITY

Many of us dream of acquiring great wealth someday. We can quit the day job, help those who need help, live life on our own terms. Still, that dream rarely comes true. Despite the availability of opportunities in this country, most of us feel bound by our career and wealth options. So many people think they are limited. They accept a life of less because they think that's the best they can do. They play the game of *At Least*. "At least I have a roof over my head." "At least we have food on the table." "At least I have a job to go to every day." They give up before they learn what I learned by experiencing many successes—and some failures as well. Sure, they wish they had more money. Yes, they'd like to be the proverbial "millionaire next door," but they don't know how to achieve that. Because they don't know how, the wish never becomes a goal. Does that mean you have to be born rich? No. I wasn't. Does it mean you have to be a genius? No again. If you've ever defaulted to the kind of thinking I've described here, this book can change that for you.

My parents gave my wife Peggy and me a trip to Bermuda for a wedding gift. That September, I was going to be a full-time student at the Wharton School at the University of Pennsylvania, and Peggy was scheduled to start her teaching position in elementary education. Although I had a summer job, I would also have to pay the rent on our new apartment upon our return. On our way to the airport the night of our wedding, my new wife and I argued in the car because I was counting the money we had received. Peggy didn't think I should be doing that, and she was probably right, but I had to know how much was there. It was all the money we had to our names.

I started with next to nothing and grew that to $10,000. After a few years, my net worth now exceeds $50 million. And no one has to pay to send Peggy and me to Bermuda anymore. We own a home there. Yet I still get a kick when I can buy a Brioni suit for ten dollars at a thrift store instead of $7,000. Money—especially saving money—should give you pleasure. But saving alone will not do it. It must be invested.

WHAT I WANT FOR YOU

Wealth is bigger than just having a bunch of money. It's what allows us to invest in our homes, our businesses, and our families. I want to make that possible for you and for as many people as I can reach with my message. In this book, I will draw upon my vast personal resources of knowledge and experience that I have accumulated over more than fifty years of advising clients and managing money. I will show you where Wall Street has gone wrong and how you can do right. I'll try to reassure you about why some of the drastic shifts in our economy following a disastrous 2020 will do what drastic shifts always do in economies and in life.

Every suggestion I make is supported with independently verifiable data, repeatedly proving that whether you are just beginning to save and invest, if your retirement is right around the corner, or if you are somewhere between those two situations, a disciplined and focused long-term investment strategy is your path to a wealthy future. We're going to see that short-term, get-rich-quick investing strategies don't work. But we'll also see how popular long-term, play-it-safe strategies can't create wealth. This book will argue that the only way to create financial security is by employing a long-term investment strategy that embraces volatility.

I have many hopes about what this book will do for you. I hope it encourages you to spend less and invest more. I hope it arms you with information about investing, the workings of Wall Street, the importance of compounding, the realities of real estate, and the truth about financial advisors. I hope it makes you dream, and I hope it makes you excited about doing everything I describe here. Most of all, I hope this book makes you think—and I truly hope it reminds you to start thinking ahead.

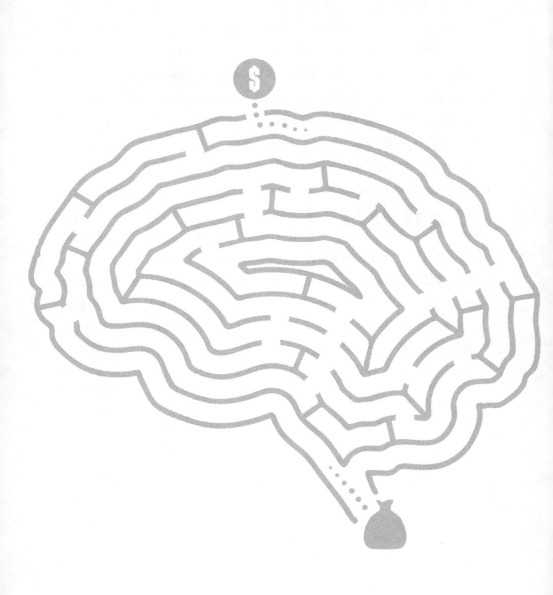

CHAPTER ONE

CHART YOUR COURSE

Curranism #1: *"When you have too much confidence, you buy anything. When you have too much fear, you don't do anything. The truth is somewhere in the middle. If things are either too bad or too good, you have to get in the middle."*

Ten years ago, I brought in an account that was worth $12 million. Pretty exciting, right? Over time, we did an excellent job with that account, and in the last six months, the clients returned and asked us to take over managing $50 million. As you may have noticed, they didn't return overnight. They watched what we could do, and they didn't yank out their money the first time they didn't like what was going on with the economy.

Building wealth is like gaining attention in the marketplace. When I look at my own career and those of my colleagues and clients, I can see that gaining attention requires three things: visibility, recognition, and respect. Anyone can be visible, and after you've accomplished that, you have to gain recognition, which is more long term. Last comes respect. Once you've achieved that, it grows over time. Money, like respect, is cumulative. You can't gain it if you're up and down and all over the place. You have to weather the circumstances out of your control and stay constant.

The term is *sustainable*, and I was using that long before it became a buzzword. If you get rich quick, chances are very good that the wealth you've acquired that way won't be sustainable. That's one reason lottery winners are more likely than other Americans to declare bankruptcy within the first three to five years after they win the millions that are supposed to change their lives.[2] More about that shortly.

SUSTAINABLE WEALTH: YOUR GOAL

Wouldn't it be great if you had a map to follow that would lead you just to the right amount of money you need to live a wealthy lifestyle? That's not going to happen until you can pinpoint what the right amount is—for you. Before you chart your financial course, you need to understand your goal. That's because there isn't just one map, but many. Some of us choose different routes, and some don't chart a course at all. Exploring the country or the backroads of your city can be fun, but when it comes to your future, a well-thought-out strategy will lead you to your goal. That means you need to know where you are starting and where you want to end up.

This is the time I have to tell you that "I want to be rich" is not a goal, although if your desire is strong enough, you may be so

---

2   Scott Hankins, Mark Hoekstra, Paige Marta Skiba, "The Ticket to Easy Street? The Financial Consequences of Winning the Lottery," *The Review of Economics and Statistics* 93, no. 3 (August 2011): 961–969, https://doi.org/10.1162/REST_a_00114.

motivated that you seek out a plan. "I want to be happy" isn't a goal either. These are generalizations. You need to get specific. As Robert Kiyosaki said, "It's not how much money you make but how much money you keep, how hard it works for you, and how many generations you keep it for."

Fortunately, even after Peggy caught me counting money on our wedding night, she decided to stick with me anyway, and when we set out on the road of life, we had specific plans. We determined what we wanted, how to go about getting it, and then we did what was necessary.

Of course, life does not always go as planned, and when it doesn't, you need to adapt. However, that's no excuse for not having a course of action. Just as is the case with a real map (including the one on your phone), you may hit a dead end or a detour. Then you readjust and start again. Because of my discipline and adaptability, I did not just meet my goals, but I exceeded them by becoming wealthier than I intended *earlier* than I expected. Still, my goal was sustainable wealth that would take care of Peggy and me and, I hoped, the generations that followed us.

I started with a dollar figure, and that's what you need to do. Some people say wealth is millions of dollars. Some define wealth as not having debt. Others say that wealth is being able to retire at a young age or travel the world or own a vacation home or drive a fancy car. You fill in the blanks. *Merriam-Webster* defines it this way:

1. abundance of valuable material possessions or resources

2. abundant supply: profusion[3]

More than anything, *wealth is being able to live your life the way you want to.*

---

[3]   *Merriam-Webster*, s.v. "wealth," https://www.merriam-webster.com/dictionary/wealth.

Let me say that again. Wealth is being able to live *your* life the way *you* want to.

Wealth is having enough money to work if you want to, to play when you want to, and to live where you want to. I believe I know what it takes to become wealthy, and furthermore, I believe just about anyone can do it. You just need a little knowledge, a lot of discipline, and you, too, can live the life you want to, not the one you must. Ultimately, wealth is freedom.

Several authors writing about financial planning try to focus individuals on what they call your "number." This is the amount of income needed in order to pay for everything your salary currently pays for, your day-to-day expenses. This not-so-magic number is how much you would need and plan to earn. Although at some point you will need to explore possible numbers and dollars, that process is only part of the equation, not the focal point.

For example, if you work for the government or for some of the older companies still in existence, you may retire with a pension. You may also receive Social Security or have an IRA. Thus, you'll be able to save less for retirement than someone who is self-employed, who does not have a pension or other sources of income to rely upon and will have to create all of his or her income from personal savings and investments.

Wealth is a number that will sustain your lifestyle without you ever having to work another day in your life.

A better number to consider is how much income you need to retire. We all want wealth, but what's the dollar figure that you attach to that? Here's my definition. Wealth is a number that will sustain your lifestyle without you ever having to work another day in your life. It allows you to make choices about your life without being limited by dollars. So it's a combination of freedom and security. In an old Kris Kristofferson song, the singer/songwriter/actor describes freedom as another word for "nothing left to lose." Poetic as that sounds, true freedom is the security of realizing that you can make decisions about your life and the way you live it because you know you will be able to meet your needs.

Your needs may vary from my needs or your best friend's needs, and that's the way it should be. Understanding those needs is what will give you the power right now to plan for them. If your dream is to live in the woods and eat what you hunt, then you can be wealthy with much less than most people. If you have a beachfront home and a $2 million lifestyle, you may need more than $50 million. A big lifestyle demands a big invested net worth to be your definition of wealthy.

Regardless of your definition or your magic number, you are going to have to factor in taxes. You also need to know how much you spend in one year for rent or mortgage, transportation or auto, food, insurance, and your gas, water, electric, and phone. You also need to look at clothing, dining, and entertainment costs. Most people have no idea of how much they'll need when they retire. That's one of the many goals I hope this book will accomplish, and that is to get you thinking about it.

Experts generally suggest you'll need about 80 percent of your preretirement income to maintain the same lifestyle in retirement, but that number varies depending on how many of your old expenses will continue with you into that retirement. If you're not working, for instance, you may no longer have to pay for lunch during the week; however, you may want to continue your gym membership or perhaps spend more money on leisure-time activities.

Later in this book, I'm going to discuss in depth what I see as the challenges of Social Security, which was intended as a supplement and not as a retirement plan. Still, you need to have a general idea of how much you will receive when the time comes. Everything changes, but as I write this book in 2020, your Social Security benefits will be based on an inflation-adjusted formula that considers the thirty-five years when you earned the highest income. That's not the only way to get a general figure though. The Social Security website will provide an estimate for you. All you need to do is create an account at www. ssa.gov. Then check out your Social Security statement, where you'll see an estimate of your future Social Security benefits based on your current income and work history.

SO WHAT'S YOUR FIGURE?

Start by calculating your net worth wealth figure. Multiply your required income by ten or eleven. Don't faint. It's just a number, and you can work toward it. Then, be honest about some important matters. How do you handle risk? That's one of the first things I evaluate when deciding how to or whether to help a client. I ask myself, *How will this person deal with volatility? How much pain can this person handle?* As we will discuss later, to invest for the benefits of long-term rewards, you have to be able to stay in. For some, 25 percent may be the maximum we need to help. That margin of discomfort—that elusive amount of savings a person can put in the stock market—is different for everyone. Know what yours is, if only so that you can sleep at night.

That margin of discomfort varies based on the times as well. After the recession, we were at the end of the get-rich-quick mania. According to the International Monetary Fund, a global recession refers to a decline in per capita world gross domestic product, supported by industrial production, trade, oil consumption, and unemployment, for a period of at least two consecutive quarters. Considering that, it's safe to say that in the United States, the Great Recession began in

December 2007. From then until it ended, the gross domestic product dropped by 4.3 percent, and the unemployment rate approached 10 percent. In short, it was a scary time for most people.

First, though, let's take a step-by-step look at that recession, often referred to as the Great Recession or the 2008 Recession.

Here's the timeline.

- Until the mid-2000s, housing prices rose, and lenders wanted to take advantage of the boom, which meant lowering qualification guidelines.

- Subprime (high-risk) mortgages were given to borrowers with poor credit histories.

- Other financial institutions acquired thousands of mortgages in bulk, usually as mortgage-backed securities, as an investment.

- The goal was a quick profit. It didn't happen.

- In February 2007, the Federal Home Loan Mortgage Corporation known as Freddie Mac said it would no longer purchase subprime mortgages or mortgage-related securities.

In April 2007, New Century Financial, a subprime mortgage lender, declared bankruptcy. They had no choice and no way to market the mortgages they owned.

In August 2007, American Home Mortgage Investment Corp. entered Chapter 11 bankruptcy. In doing so, it became the second major mortgage lender to break under the pressure of the declining housing market and the subprime financial crisis.

Young people watched this happen. Even if they didn't quite understand the reasons for the decline, they felt the impact. I believe that's why a lot of millennials today are driven by fear. They've seen their parents lose their houses, their kids' college funds, even their marriages. So your personal margin is partially sociological—what's going on in the country and the world right now—and partially psychological. Thinking about that will help as you learn more of what I'm going to share with you in this book.

Wherever you are today, you can start right now, or using my approach, you can increase what you're already doing. As you start planning, know that earlier is better, but you're never too old to plan and improve. You could already be retired but have not done as much preparation as you wish you had, but you can start putting my practices into effect regardless of your age or situation. The sooner the better is true, but never is worse. Doing nothing leads to nothing. If you start applying the outlook advice in this book, you can change the way you've been thinking about money for a lifetime. That's one of my goals for you, to change the way you think about spending, saving, and investing.

This next rule may seem like a no-brainer, but ask yourself how many times you've ignored it. Once you stop and pay attention, you will see your life change. You'll see yourself pass up ideas that sounded promising or exciting. You'll recognize them as the distractions they are, and you'll continue focusing on your goal. So why are you spending your money on momentary pleasures and not as an investment in your future? Maybe because you don't understand what spending money—a dollar, even a penny—is all about. A major part of my approach is what I'm going to share with you next, and until you master it, you will be scrambling for a plan that works for you.

YOU CAN SPEND A DOLLAR ONLY ONCE

Think about that for a moment. Only once.

Take out a dollar from your wallet, spread it out before you, and think about what it represents. One hundred pennies? Twenty nickels?

Ten dimes? Four quarters? Two fifty-cent pieces? Not that exciting, right? Easy to spend and easy to ignore until you think about all that dollar can represent for you down the road.

Remember the client I mentioned earlier who wanted to know if he should spend $20,000 of his inherited $200,000 to buy a truck? He did not understand what I want to share with you: you can spend that dollar only one time. Think of it as a seed you don't get to plant once you trade it for something else. What would you have done if you had $200,000 and wanted to buy that truck? Or what would you have done if a relative had needed $10,000 or $20,000 of that money to get out of a financial bind? (Believe me, once you have that kind of money, people who need part of it will instantly surface.)

"What choice do I have?" you might say. "This is a family member, and she/he needs help."

My question is this: Who's going to help *you* down the road? Once that dollar leaves your possession, it is gone, and its potential to multiply for you and the help you can give any family member is terminated. You haven't just lost the money you paid for the truck or gave to the person who needs it right now. No. You've also lost the wealth and security that money could have brought you in the future.

That $20,000 for a truck might not have looked like much compared to $200,000, but as you already know, truly accessing the value of money means not looking at its current worth but looking at its future worth. In order to grow wealth, time is more important than the amount. Just know that fifty cents here and a dollar there will grow over time to more than you can imagine right now, while you're spending it ordering lattes and burgers at the drive-through.

SAVING TO SPEND

Are you old enough to remember the popularity of the old Christmas clubs? I certainly am. I must have been about ten years old, watching my mom stuff dollar bills in that little bankbook in which she kept track of every dollar she spent. I can still recall how excited and motivated Mom was by the idea of all the gifts she could give my sister and me when December rolled around, and she got that money out.

The first known Christmas club began in 1909, when the treasurer of the Carlisle Trust Company, Merkel Landis, launched the club, gaining more than 350 members. Each member participated by saving twenty-eight dollars each, which was disbursed on December 1 to aid their Christmas shopping.[4] This was a special program for Native American schoolchildren, who brought in a few pennies a week and received a check at year-end. The clubs that followed were essentially forced savings programs, with coupon books to encourage

---

4   Jason Fernando, "Christmas Club," Investopedia, 2020, https://www. investopedia.com/terms/c/christmasclub.asp.

the regular payments. The coupons also encouraged regular visits to the bank, which gave the clubs an appealing social function and made them popular with banks as traffic builders.[5]

The clubs reached the height of their popularity in the 1970s for several reasons. Those accounts had a higher annual percentage yield than typical savings accounts, they had lower requirements for getting in, they had a shorter holding period, and most importantly to those like my mother who used them, they forced the individual to save. To a point, that is. Think of all the willpower that went into the hard work of saving all year. Think about the satisfaction of being able to withdraw those funds around December 1 and then taking that money—and spending it.

Whoever came up with that idea must have understood our pretty much universal need for instant gratification, and that person (or persons) was brilliant to market it as a savings account because, of course, the Christmas club concept wasn't *saving* at all. It was *saving to spend*. If you save money so you can spend it elsewhere, that's zero return.

However, the Christmas club appealed to people, especially women, most of whom, like my mother, were already trying to juggle dollars for extra expenses, including holidays. Remember, too, in those days women were, if they were lucky, getting a small allowance from their husbands, usually in cash, with the expectation that the money would be spent for groceries and other household necessities.

Imagine this. Your mother loves the Christmas club. She puts money into an account for one year, and at the end of that year, she has a significant amount—whatever that means to her. If she invests that amount, it may grow and offer her many options in the future.

---

5   S.J. Diamond, "Christmas Club Accounts Have Lost the Magic," *Los Angeles Times,* Nov. 27, 1987, https://www.latimes.com/archives/la-xpm-1987-11-27-fi-16712-story.html.

If she doesn't, she has only the money she has saved that year, which will be gone once the holidays have passed.

THINKING ABOUT MONEY

This might be a good time to examine how people think about money. Behavioral economist Richard Thaler uses the term "mental accounting" to describe how we put our money in different emotional accounts based on the way we earned it, how easily we can access it, how long we've had it, and other factors. Mental accounting greatly affects the way we spend and invest. People make these mental accounts as a way of controlling their money, by placing more worth on one type than another.

They also think of "bad" debt and "good" debt. So, maybe you pay a little extra toward your mortgage because you feel better about your home than the money you owe on, say, a credit card. You feel more positive about spending money on that debt because you want to pay off your home one day, and you feel you'll have something once that home is paid off. Your credit card, on the other hand, is just a reminder that you spent money you didn't have on something you may or may not even care about anymore. You might not even remember what you're paying off; it's just a number on the debit side of your bank account.

You probably know where I'm going with this, and the word is *interest*. You may be paying far more interest on your credit card than you are on your mortgage—probably double-digit interest. Your rational brain knows that money isn't good or bad and that loans with the highest interest should be prioritized over those with lower interest or even over low-interest saving accounts. But when it comes to money, most of us don't always listen to our rational brains.

According to Thaler, people think of value in relative rather than absolute terms. They derive pleasure not just from an object's value but also the quality of the deal—its transaction utility. In addition, humans often fail to fully consider opportunity costs (trade-offs) and are susceptible to the sunk cost fallacy; that is when they continue a behavior or endeavor as a result of previously invested resources (time, money, or effort.)[6] That's why winning the lottery may feel as if they have accumulated "free money" that they don't need to guard as they might a weekly paycheck. It's why they are willing to pay more for an event with a credit card than they would with cash.

Thaler uses the following examples:

1. Mr. and Mrs. L and Mr. and Mrs. H went on a fishing trip in the northwest and caught some salmon. They packed the fish and sent it home on an airline, but the fish were lost in transit. They received $300 from the airline. The couples take the money, go out to dinner, and spend $225. They had never spent that much at a restaurant before.

2. Mr. X is up fifty dollars in a monthly poker game. He has a queen high flush and calls a ten-dollar bet. Mr. Y owns one hundred shares of IBM which went up two today and is even in the poker game. He has a king high flush, but he folds. When X wins, Y thinks to himself, "If I had been up fifty dollars, I would have called too."

3. Mr. and Mrs. J have saved $15,000 toward their dream vacation home. They hope to buy the home in five years. The money earns 10 percent in a money market account. They just bought a new car for $11,000, which they financed with a three-year car loan at 15 percent.

---

6   "Mental accounting," Behavioral Economics, https://www.behavioraleco-nomics.com/resources/mini-encyclopedia-of-be/mental-accounting/.

4. Mr. S admires a $125 cashmere sweater at the department store. He declines to buy it, feeling that it is too extravagant. Later that month he receives the same sweater from his wife for a birthday present. He is very happy. Mr. and Mrs. S have only joint bank accounts.

Each of these anecdotes illustrates a type of behavior where a mental accounting system induces an individual to violate a simple economic principle.[7]

When a company offers its employees retirement plans that include no option for investing in their own company's stock, they typically put half of their money to bonds and half to stocks. But when they were given the option to invest in their own company's stock, they allocated more than 40 percent of their money to company stock and divided the rest equally between stocks and bonds. In other words, almost three-fourths of their portfolio was now in equities for the simple reason that they put their own company's stock in a *different mental account* than other equity investments.[8]

> **Money is just that: money— not good, not bad, just a tool to help you get where you want to go in life.**

The Christmas clubs took advantage of that concept of mental accounting. Those accounts, especially to women of limited means, took on a special meaning, and the money they contained was special, too, because it was earmarked for a specific purpose, one of utmost importance to the person doing the "saving." It had all the emotional

---

7   Richard Thaler, "Mental Accounting & Consumer Choice," *Marketing Science* 4, no. 3 (Summer 1985), 199–214.

8   James Surowiecki, "Bitter Money & Christmas Clubs," *Forbes*, Feb. 14, 2006, https://www.forbes.com/2006/02/11/mental-accounting-surow-iecki_cz_js_money06_0214surowiecki.html#1e567919f203

trappings: the special bankbook, the statements. No one stopped to think that they could just put their extra dollars in a jar and have the same effect because they would not have had the same emotional effect.

Economic principles are sound. The way we think about money is not always so sound. It's based on emotion, temperament, personal history, and perceived *needs*, which may be *wants* that are traveling incognito. One of my goals in writing this book is to help you look at money as just that—not a salve to ease the wrongs in your life, not as something that was easy to come and should be easy to go (as my client felt the money spent on that new truck should be). Money is just that: money—not good, not bad, just a tool to help you get where you want to go in life. I hope that as you move through this book, I can convince you why and how you should hang onto those dollars and put them to work for you.

WHAT'S YOUR WHY?

I'm sure you've heard this question before, and if you haven't heard it from your financial advisor, you may have a problem. Many use this question in terms of what someone wants in life, their reason for being, and indeed, their purpose.

KNOWING YOUR WHY

- provides clarity

- keeps you focused

- fuels your passion

- helps you find meaning in setbacks and develop your resilience

- defines and helps you remain true to your core values

I use this question when I talk about money. Whenever I speak with a client, I ask them, "What are you investing for?"

Sometimes I get a strange look. The obvious answers are "To get rich," or "To save for retirement," or "Because I must." But successful investing requires much more than just general categories of purpose. The more you know why you are investing, the more likely you are to be disciplined to stick to your savings and investing plan when the markets and your personal life challenge your resolve.

Your goals need to be specific and elaborate. Saying, "I want to save for retirement," is not enough. When you retire, where do you want to live? What kind of home do you want to own or rent? Or do you want to live in a condo, on an island or a boat? In what kind of activities do you want to engage? Travel? Golf? Exploring great restaurants? Getting involved in and contributing to causes you care about?

If you are younger and saving for your first house, you must state what you want specifically, not what you think you can get. Whether it is a vacation or your child's tuition, you need to be specific.

These goals are important because rather than save and hope, which will likely not get you where you really want to be, you can focus your efforts and make decisions in your life progressively—about your career, investments, and lifestyle—that may affect your success in reaching your financial goals. Without specific and detailed goals, attaining any degree of financial security will be difficult, if not impossible.

German philosopher Friedrich Nietzsche said, "He who has a why can endure any *how*." Once you have your *why*, that is, your true goal and your true reason for that goal, the *how* will become essential to you, not just another chore you have to complete. Knowing your why is also important so that you don't slip into emotional decisions and so that you have the motivation to work hard.

IT TAKES COMMITMENT

Here's another truth about wealth. If you really want it, you're going to have to commit to it. I learned this lesson at an early age when I was playing high school sports. I was a pretty good athlete, and I took my talent in sports for granted. Once I was competing on the soccer team, I realized I had been wrong. Other players were giving it all they had, and I was not. It showed

I didn't forget that, though, and with my first job, when everyone else was working from nine to five, I worked seven to five and much later. In fact, they finally had to give me a key to the front door. At first, though, I had to enter where the trucks came through. In fact, Gus the garbage man (he calls himself a garbologist) was my first client. I still manage his investments today.

Boxer Mike Tyson said, "Everybody has a plan until they get punched in the mouth." During the financial crisis following the coronavirus pandemic of 2020, a lot of people—maybe you—felt as if they had been punched in the mouth. There went the 401(k). There went the emergency fund. And for too many, especially those in services such as the beauty and restaurant industries, there went the job.

While we're quoting people, here's one from Harry Truman that still rings true today: "It's a recession when your neighbor loses his job. It's a depression when you lose yours." So, the way we analyze any economic condition is from our own home base. If you're an employee, you are going to worry in a close, narrow way. Basically, you wonder *if*, and if so, *how long* you'll be paid. If you're an employer, as I am, you have to worry about your employees' paychecks, your paycheck, and the business that keeps those paychecks coming. This is true all the time but especially so during a national economic crisis.

If you are a police officer, you are a police officer in good times and in bad. If you are a TV newscaster, you remain one in good times and in bad. The way you do your job might change; the small details might shift. But you still are who you are. If you are an investor, you are an investor in good times and in bad. That's what I am.

On Tuesday, November 24, 2020, The Dow Jones Industrial Average closed above 30,000 for the first time, extending an eight-month rebound, putting the Dow up 62 percent from its March low.

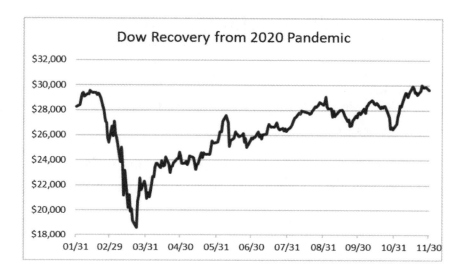

Dow Recovery from 2020 Pandemic

"The real learning lesson over the last decade is you just put your head down. You don't try to time the market; you take advantage of weakness," Dev Kantesaria, a managing partner at Valley Forge Capital Management, told *The Wall Street Journal*.[9]

The biggest leaps and bounds companies make are during times like the ones we just lived through. Our company experienced record growth. Yes, the way I'm doing my job has changed. Even my location initially changed. But nothing destroyed who I am or what I do. Here are some basic lessons I'd like to share for investing in good and not-so-good times.

---

9   Gunjan Banerji, Akane Otani, and Michael Wursthorn. "Behind Dow 30000: A Self-Perpetuating Upward Spiral," *The Wall Street Journal*, Nov. 25, 2020.

THIS IS WHERE YOU START

- Plan for sustainable wealth.

- Remember that you can spend that dollar of yours only once.

- Don't give into mental accounting (including the dead-end Christmas clubs or anything similar).

- Know your *why*.

- Commit to your goal and work toward it.

We all have ideas about how we'd like investing to work. As I mentioned before, some of us are risk averse and don't want any volatility. Others try to play Wall Street's lopsided game and day-trade. Maybe you are one of those who thinks Wall Street is the answer. Maybe, however, the very mention of that place makes you uneasy. Well, don't be, because right now, I'm going to show you the truth about Wall Street and its short-term strategies.

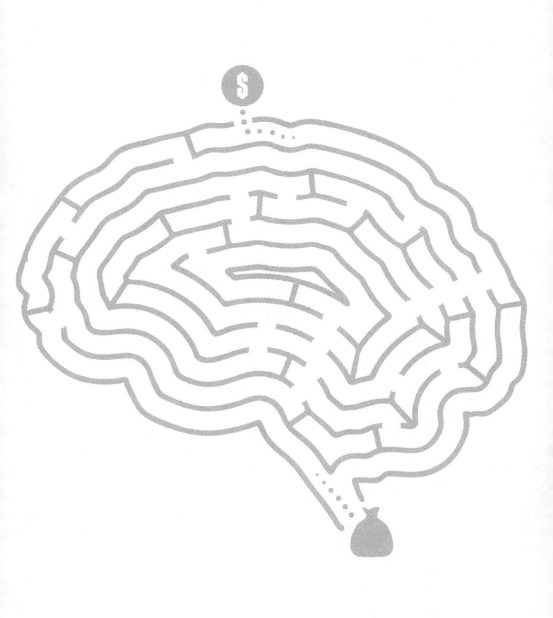

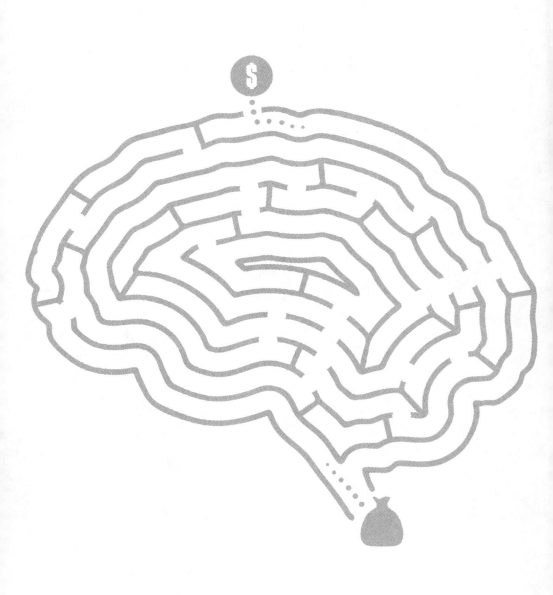

CHAPTER TWO

PERCEPTION AND REALITY

Curranism #2: *"Don't underestimate yourself. Don't overestimate others."*

Knock, knock, knock. You open your front door, and there stands a vacuum cleaner salesperson, who then proceeds to show you the Super Sweeper of the Century. This vacuum cleaner, the salesperson tells you, can do everything but cook your breakfast. Yes, it's a little pricey, but what would you expect from a machine that's going to forever change your life?

So you buy the machine, and six weeks pass. Weeks, not months. One day, at your front door, you hear a familiar sound. *Knock, knock, knock.*

That's right. Same salesperson, different machine. This one is the Super Sweeper of the Universe, and unlike that dog of a machine you bought six weeks ago, this one can actually cook breakfast *and* wash the dishes.

Welcome to Wall Street.

Before I go any further, I think it's important to say that I'm not anti-Wall Street, and I'm not going to waste your time bashing any institution. My goal in this book is to help you invest to get rich, and that means showing you how things work.

Wall Street and I go way back. I was in high school when I knew I wanted to make money, and I knew college was a means to an end. I was on the five-year co-op program at Drexel University in Philadelphia, and after the second year, I could work six months, and my experience was to be in the investment business.

"Do you know anyone with money?" my professor asked me. "If you're going to be in the investment business, you need someone to sell your products to." In the 1960s, that's how it was. Still, at the age of twenty-two, I knew I wanted to be in the financial services business.

Next I tried to get hired by a major Wall Street firm, Hayden Stone, which had been around since the 1890s. I was attracted to them, and they seemed attracted to me, which is probably why I wanted them to offer me a job. The first day I arrived for work, they told me that the New York Stock Exchange had sanctioned Hayden Stone and shut down its training program. They would still train me, however. I went back to my old job with the New York State Department of Transportation. When they were approved to hire and train new brokers, I went back.

I did my initial stockbroker training with seventy other young people in New York City. In those early days of investment management, no one trained you to be an investor. They trained you to be a salesperson, investing probably as much time in you as the Super Sweeper of the Century invested in the guy selling vacuums. My own training took just six months. Today no training is required. The only requirement is to pass a test.

After those six months, they gathered the seventy of us in a conference hall for a closing ceremony and asked each of us to stand up and tell the people in the room how we were going to make money for our clients.

My answer was simple. "I won't."

"What?" I'm sure my trainer wasn't pleased, but I'd been asked a question, and I was going to answer it. "I can't make money for my clients," I said. "Not as long as I have to make sales." I went on to explain that if I had to sell first—and clearly I did—I would wind up giving people what they wanted—not what they needed.

And to this day, that's still the Wall Street tradition.

Even though I knew next to nothing at the time, that was the way I perceived Wall Street and investing. Now, fifty-five years after the fact, I am reaping rewards.

Six months after I started, I was registered and trained, and Hayden Stone was bankrupt. They were eventually sold to a firm called Cogan, Berlind, Weill & Levitt. Other jobs followed for me, and although I was a sales star who made the president's council the first year, putting me in the top 10 percent based on sales, I was dissatisfied. I was making money, but my clients were not doing as well.

As I said at the start of this chapter, I am not anti-Wall Street. I just want to point out that Wall Street gets paid—just as those seventy other trainees and I did—on what, not how, they are doing right now. Long-term results are not part of their income. Sales are now.

Furthermore, the interests of Wall Street have never been more distant from those of investors today. Wall Street wants action right now. The next ten years is a lifetime away, and long-term investing doesn't offer enough to motivate Wall Street. As someone said to me years ago, it's like planting a garden or a tree and pulling it up after a few months to see what's wrong with it. With that approach, you're never going to get much, and very little of what you planted will come to fruition.

TIME, NOT TIMING

As Gordon Gekko said in *Wall Street*, "Money never sleeps, pal." But that fact worries people; it makes them anxious. Fear and greed are the two biggest emotions that destroy people's financial decision-making.

The interests of Wall Street have never been more distant from those of investors today.

A bull market, as you probably know, is a time when stock prices are rising and market sentiment is optimistic. A bull market generally occurs when there is a rise of 20 percent or more in a broad market index. A bear market occurs when stock prices are declining and market sentiment is pessimistic. A bear market occurs when a broad market index falls by 20 percent.

With a bull market, investor sentiment turns to excitement, and they might learn about investments from news stories, friends, coworkers, or family and be enticed to test new waters. The excitement might even lead the investor to try to obtain gains from investments that are emerging because of bullish market conditions.[10]

Bull markets, such as the one in the late 1990s during the dot-com boom, encourage greed. But greed isn't money; it's emotion, and investors fueled more buying by raising prices to excessive levels. When that bubble burst, stock prices remained about the same during

---

10   "Bull Market," Investor, https://www.investor.gov/introduction-investing/
       investing-basics/glossary/bull-market.

2000–2009. In March 2009, the great bull market emerged and continues through 2021. Too many investors remain only partially invested in stocks because they still do not have confidence. They remain fearful. Meanwhile, at this writing, stocks are up six-fold.

This get-rich-quick thinking makes it hard to maintain a disciplined long-term investment plan, especially amid what Federal Reserve chairman Alan Greenspan famously called "irrational exuberance."

The key to successful investment is not about timing. It is about time. Wall Street, of course, is about timing, not so different from that salesperson knock-knock-knocking on your front door.

Overall, if I had to comment on one aspect of Wall Street and investing, it is this. People get too caught up in the moment. Talking heads start saying a company—Apple, perhaps—has problems. "Sell it," the talking heads advise. Then guess what happens next. Panic, that's what.

"Apple loses 64 billion in stock value as Wall Street is in 'full panic mode' on iPhone demand," stated a *USA Today* article.[11]

"Apple Stock Could Crash and Take the Broader Market Down Too," was the title of a *CCN* article, which would go on to say, "The S&P 500 is market cap-weighted, meaning the more valuable a company is, the more of an effect it has on the S&P 500—the index most commonly used as a proxy for the entire stock market."[12]

---

11   Tae Kim, "Apple loses $64 billion in stock value as Wall Street is in 'full panic mode' on iPhone demand," *USA Today*, April 24, 2018, https://www.usatoday.com/story/tech/2018/04/24/apple-loses-64-billion-stock-value-wall-street-full-panic-mode-iphone-demand/546707002/.

12   Lawrence Meyers, "Apple's Stock Could Crash and Take the Broader Market Down Too," CCN, May 30, 2019, https://www.ccn.com/apple-stock-crash-stock-market-down/.

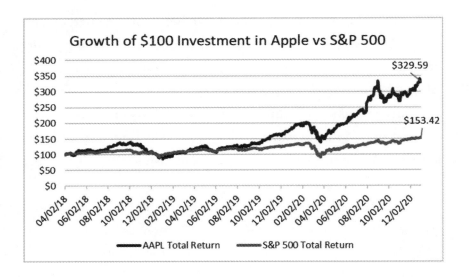

Growth of $100 Investment in Apple vs S&P 500

"*Sell it*" becomes the mantra of the panicked. When you're panicked, you sell, and you create more panic. Pretty soon, you have a self-fulfilling prophecy.

Back to the garden analogy again. If you plant a garden, you want to watch it grow, but you also know—and this is key—that there's a time frame, and like it or not, you have to wait. If a storm is coming, pulling up that plant and shoving it into a pot inside your house isn't going to guarantee much of a harvest.

THE PARABLE OF THE PENNY

Great crashes are part of our history. The Panic of 1857 started when the ship the SS *Central America*, carrying passengers and gold, was lost in a hurricane. This caused panic among banks that needed this gold; investors who were suffering heavy losses in the stock market; railroads, which were also losing money; and land speculators, who were expecting new railroad routes to be constructed. The panic led to a severe economic depression in the United States that lasted almost three years and increased tension in the United States, which was on the brink of a civil war.

Yet we survived.

Although the Wall Street crash of 1929 was not the only cause of the Great Depression, it hastened the economic collapse. During the 1920s, the stock market expanded rapidly. After wild speculation, it reached its peak that August, along with rising unemployment and declining production. On October 29 of that year—Black Tuesday—investors traded 16 million shares on the New York Stock Exchange, and billions of dollars were lost. By 1933, almost 50 percent of banks in the United States had failed, and almost 30 percent of the workforce was unemployed.

Yet we survived.

Also known as Flash Crash of 1962, the Kennedy Slide of 1962 refers to the stock market decline from December 1961 to June 1962 during John F. Kennedy's presidency. Although a change in investor confidence (panic) is often blamed for the crash, factors contributing to that included inflated stock prices. However, only a year and two months after bottoming out, market indexes hit new highs.

Yet again we survived.

Now I want you to think about a penny, any penny. Maybe you have one lying around. How much money would one penny have earned for you today if one of your ancestors had invested it in 1776?

How much do you think a penny invested in 1776 would be worth today if it had been invested for the long term? Of course, it would depend on the rate of return. Perhaps even more importantly, it would have required tremendous faith in the future for the original states.

Let's say a distant relative of yours invested it to earn 2 percent. Honestly, why bother? That relative of yours might as well have spent it, because it would be worth only $1.23 in 243 years.

Fear always seems to win. And if not fear, spending will consume the investment long before it can grow to meaningful amounts.

Suppose it had been invested to earn 4 percent. Again, we would agree it would probably have been a good decision if it had simply been spent, because it would only be worth $137.75.

When we get the return up to about 6 percent, the value would be $14,103, but even that is not enough to buy a new car in 2021.

It starts to get interesting when the rate of return is 8 percent. Then the penny would be worth $1,324,257.93.

But that investment achieves an amazing number at a 10 percent return. The value would be $114,399,069.88. Never forget the long-term return in stocks is about 10 percent.

PENNY VERSUS PEOPLE

Instead of pitting that penny against people, let's clarify and make it penny versus human nature. Based on what I have learned about human behavior, the chance of multiple generations holding the investment for 243 years is about zero. If the American Revolution were not enough to scare the holder into selling, I am sure something else along the way to $114,399,069 would. One big event would have been the Civil War. I think we will agree that holding a penny invested in 1776 for 243 years would never have happened. The human species is simply not wired to have enough faith and confidence. Fear always seems to win. And if not fear, spending will consume the investment long before it can grow to meaningful amounts.

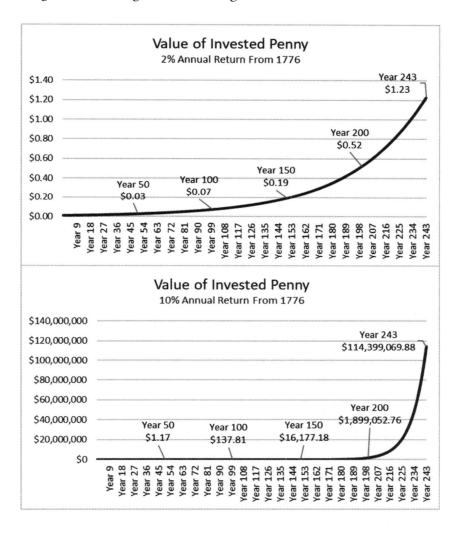

The S&P index began in 1926, and the annual average return is about 10 percent. The 10 percent hypothetical return I used in my penny example is based on almost one hundred years of actual stock market returns measured by the S&P, so the return isn't a fantasy; human willpower to hang onto that investment probably is.

In his book *Stocks for the Long Run*, Jeremy Siegel wrote that $1 million invested in 1801 with dividends reinvested would have grown to $8.8 trillion by 2001. In terms of purchasing power, $1 million in 1801 would be worth about $15 million in 2001. I feel safe in saying that most people would not have had that much money, but wealthy landholders and industrialists would have. $1 million in 1801 was the equivalent of .04 percent of total wealth in the United States.

Total wealth in the stock market does not accumulate as fast as the total return index (S&P 500) would indicate. Then (and now), investors consume most of their dividends and capital gains.

SKEPTICISM IS FINE

You may or may not agree that stocks have been a wonderful place to invest. Many are skeptical about returns going back to 1802, and there are many good reasons to be skeptical. Keep in mind, however, that scholars who criticize the assumed rate of 10 percent since 1802 argue it is overstated by as much as 2 percent. Let's agree not to quibble. Does it really matter to us if the number is 9 percent or 10 percent? Or let's say even 8 percent?

So that little penny your ancestor invested would have survived the great disasters that send others scrambling. As we're even more aware of in our post-2020 world, disasters will happen. They have happened, and they continue to happen, and we can seldom predict them. That doesn't mean we're powerless though. What matters is how we approach and plan for them.

When I'm in Albany, on my way to the office, I frequently stop at McDonald's, where I have coffee with the regulars, and often our conversations turn to investing. Here's what I take away about those people from many of our conversations. They worry. A lot.

If the stock market is going up, that's a major worry because maybe it's then going to go down. If the stock market is going down, that's a major worry because how long is it going to stay down? The stock market goes up, and it goes down. If you don't know what you're going to do when that happens, you're in trouble.

"What if the market goes down?" people ask me. That's the fear with which most investors try to cope because, of course, the market will go down. It did that as I was writing this book. Yet that anxiety and stress make it difficult to understand what that money is going to do over the years. Try not to think of life and investing in the short term. The simple fact is if you are too cautious and too worried, you won't lose, but you won't win either.

I wasn't born knowing this, but I had a desire to learn it, and now it's part of me, as I hope it will be part of you after you read and think about what I share with you in this book.

HAVE A PLAN

One way to ease the fear is having a plan. Here's an example of how we never know what's going to happen at any particular time. A couple of years ago, I flew to San Diego to speak to a group of interventional radiologists, and I had carefully prepared my twenty-minute talk. Just as I was ready to start speaking, the audio-visual system had a glitch, and as the technician came up to fix it, I stepped off the riser, missed the three steps, and fell. All I can say about that is if you're going to fall off a stage, do it in a room of physicians. A swarm of them headed straight for me.

The other thing I can say about it is this. I had a plan—twenty minutes and a message to deliver. Was I shaken? Of course. Was I embarrassed? I'm sure I must have been. But I had a plan. I got back on the riser and delivered my message.

Have you ever watched a gymnast? I'm always amazed by the way that, when they make a mistake, as every gymnast does, they immediately regain their composure. Ice skaters are equally fast to react because they are anticipating that things may not always go that smoothly for them. They aren't hoping against hope. They aren't refusing to compete because it's too unpredictable. They are planning ahead, and when something unforeseen happens, they return their focus to the now. The same is true of investing. You know much of the day-to-day is out of your control. So in order to achieve the best results, you must have a plan and stick to it.

When people are fearful and stressed, they are looking for hope, which makes them vulnerable. Wall Street often tries to pacify us with the safest investment. Think back to the vacuum salesperson having the nerve to come back six weeks later with a new product. The new product may not be the best product long term. Evaluating stocks—and people—takes time. Not all stocks, not all companies are the same.

Let's head back to my morning coffee stop for a moment. When you stop at McDonald's, you do so because you are strapped for time and maybe money. You don't expect a gourmet hamburger or a five-course meal. You do expect, and you receive, a high degree of certainty. Everything tastes the same every time.

THE RECIPE FOR SUCCESS

There's a difference between speculation and trying to make money quickly. Cheap stocks don't get you quality for the long term. When you look at stocks, you need to tune out the sales pitch of anyone who's going to make money selling that stock to you—especially if that person tried to sell you the stock version of a vacuum cleaner not long before.

Here's what you should look for:

- a company with little or no debt

- a company that is well managed

- a company with a solid history of growth

We'll come back to this repeatedly in the book because it's crucial and because not everything that looks the same is the same. If we look at several individuals—where they live, what kind of cars they drive, their earnings over a year—they might all look the same. But if, at the end of ten or twenty years, we looked at a balance sheet, we would see that they are not the same at all. We'd easily see which individuals were raising their earnings and, while doing that, were building net worth with little or no debt. That's the recipe for success. When we find that company, that's where we invest.

SHORT-TERM HOPE

Just as an individual can mislead you with all the trappings of wealth, Wall Street, advertising, and advisors with personal gain in mind can entice you into thinking you're getting something you're not. It's easy to deny reality when the pitch you're getting—the pitch that will make money for someone else right now—can be so much more appealing than the promise of what your money will earn for you years from now.

When you deal with Wall Street, you have to think about their objectives versus your objectives. Wall Street talks about what *it* makes, not what it makes for its *clients*. It pounds its chest like King Kong and talks about what it has done. Still, it's not about how many clients they have but how much they are earning for those clients. Wall Street's objective is to make money. Our objective—yours and mine—is for us to make money. It's about us as individuals.

As a rule, Wall Street makes more money than its customers do, something I was figuring out back in those early months of my career. Wall Street doesn't own long term what it's selling, but it gets paid selling it to you. They do that, in part, by selling you short-term hope. So you have to think about their objectives versus your objectives.

Wall Street is short term. You need to think about where you need to be throughout your life. That is not about what you can collect right now but about where you are today and how much time you have to start using what you've stored.

LONG TERM, NOT SHORT TERM

People tend to invest when their confidence is at its highest. Yet the time to invest is when you feel the least confident. In a piece I wrote in the depths of the recent financial crisis, I pointed out that in the crises that had preceded this one, the market always recovered rapidly and in a sustainable fashion. If you know you use a lot of paper towels, and if you can buy them at 40 percent off, why wouldn't you do that and stock up? If you believe in your heart in the long-term viability that the market is going to average 10 percent, why would you ever consider selling? I've built my career on that belief, through good and not-so-good times, not to mention more than one financial crisis.

On Wall Street, nearly everyone's selling you short-term investment strategies. That's not because short-term strategies work. It's because people pushing those strategies get paid in the short term. Unfortunately for them, their rewards and their clients will be short term as well. When you are dealing with other people's money, I strongly believe it must be designed to achieve the client's long-term needs. The short term is irrelevant.

From the beginning, I always understood there was a consequence in everything I did and every choice I made. I was always thinking what the cost was going to be. One of the things I realized along the way was I could do whatever I had to, but I wasn't building a foundation. Only in the later stages of my career did I realize how many years I spent in order to know what I'm talking about. I had to learn a lot along the way, and I did. One of the most important things I learned is that if you're going to be honest, first you have to be honest with yourself. It's not "*do as I say.*" It must be "*do as I do.*" That's probably one reason I never ask an assistant to get coffee or a sandwich for me. There may have been one or two times, but they truly were exceptions. Whatever made me announce at my first hiring ceremony that I couldn't make money for my clients if I were selling them has driven my career.

In many cases, it's not that that old metaphorical vacuum cleaner with which I started this chapter didn't work. It just needed *time* to work. Think about that, and imagine what would happen if you simply held on to that purchase and watched how it evolved with time.

HOW YOU SHOULD LOOK AT THE STOCK MARKET

- Remember that Wall Street gets paid for what they're doing right now, not five or ten years from now.

- Don't worry if the market is up or down; have a plan.

- Look for a company with little or no debt that is able to build equity.

- Evaluate stocks as you do individuals who may look the same in the short term, but they vary greatly in the long term.

- Be suspicious if someone tries to get you to invest in something that sounds too good to be true.

- Ask yourself why Wall Street makes more money than its customers do.

- Know that Wall Street gets paid by selling to *you*.

- And ultimately, despite what the talking heads may be telling you, remember that successful investing is about time, *not* timing.

With that, I'd like to share with you my approach to investing, one that is all about time, one that is proven, and one that I'm convinced can make you very wealthy—not right now, but when you most need that wealth. I'd like to start, though, with talking a little more about your outlook regarding money. It can start early in your life, as it did in mine, or later in your life. Younger is better, but all that matters is that you change the way you think about money as soon as possible.

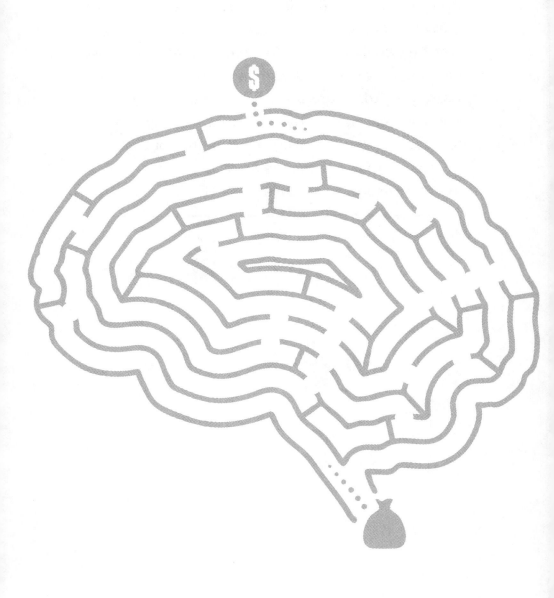

CHAPTER THREE

THE INVESTOR'S OUTLOOK

Curranism #3: *"Opportunity knocks all the time. The problem is we just don't hear."*

My grandfather died when he was in his early sixties. My mother was diabetic with high blood pressure. She insisted that I go through a battery of tests in the college hospital for a three-day period, and the message I heard loudly and clearly from her (although she didn't say it in these words) was, "Don't be like we are. Don't be like I am."

This was the late 1950s. After all those tests, the doctor told me something that got my attention, which is why I can remember it word-for-word today.

"Tom, we don't know too much about diabetes and heart disease, but we do know that the leaner we are, the more likely it is that we won't have them."

At the time, I weighed 205 pounds. I immediately got down to 178 pounds, which is where I am today. I grew up hearing people say, "I could've done this" or "I should've done that." I didn't want to be one of those people, and quite frankly, considering my family history, I was worried.

My outlook is the investor's outlook. How we look at life, money, and investing is shaped by emotions, which are shaped, positively or negatively, by our early experiences. As I pointed out before, fear and greed are two big emotions that destroy people's financial decision-making. Since embarking on this book, I've thought a great deal about fear, and I've decided that, as dangerous and distracting as it may be, it is preferable to stress. Here's why. Fear drives us to action, just the way fear of ending up like my grandfather drove me to get tested and to lose weight.

Stress creates inaction about what we cannot control and blocks us from taking action about what we can control.

On the other hand, stress is worrying about what we should do. Stress creates inaction about what we cannot control and blocks us from taking action about what we can control. That's why I think stress is worse than fear. When we take away fear, we take away the compulsion to act. Let's face it. Sometimes you have to act. You can't let fear force you into dangerous decisions, however.

If I had let fear of being like my grandfather drive me to some bizarre diet or the neighborhood bar, I would have been in trouble. Instead, thanks to my mother, I sought out the opinion of an expert—

the doctor—who, after analyzing the data, gave me his professional advice. I didn't question the advice; I didn't go off looking for someone who would tell me something I wanted to hear or who would promise me that I was perfectly healthy at my current weight. I followed that advice and never looked back.

That's also a wise approach to investing. Talk to an expert who will examine your personal data and give you suggestions. Then, based on your comfort level, follow those suggestions.

PROACTIVE, NOT REACTIVE

You have to know what you will do before it happens, or you'll panic. You have to anticipate and plan. Otherwise you'll react, which is frequently not good. When we react, we tend to think more than knee jerk.

Let's suppose you're in the middle of something very important, and your spouse or your child interrupts you with a personal problem. It happens, right? You shouldn't be shocked, yet when your attention is elsewhere, it's easy to react without thinking. Well, you have to know what you're going to do before that happens, or you might say something you'll later regret. In my own life, if I don't know what I'm going to do in a given situation, I've tried to train my mind so that I don't do anything. I'm always giving feedback to myself, trying to analyze how I should have reacted rather than saying somebody pushed my buttons. People don't push your buttons; you allow your buttons to be pushed.

Having patience is a universal rule. Impatience, anger, and frustration can ruin your investment plan. They are not options to be exercised.

Here's how that relates to investing. People are either proactive or reactive. Someone proactive takes action, and someone who is reactive is just responding to a situation, usually not in a way that serves them best. But when you are proactive, you already know what you'll do if something unexpected happens. You already have confidence in your investment decision because you've thought it out. If I bought a company and it went down 10, 20, or even 30 percent within twenty-four hours after the time I bought it, I would not do anything except buy more. That's right; I would not question my decision.

As I mentioned before, I would have already spent considerable time before buying to focus on the most important variables. That would include the company's level of debt, which normally would be somewhere between zero and no more than 35 percent. I'd also want to see earnings growth rates over a five-year period of 10 percent or greater. Further, I would have been looking for companies that reinvest in themselves and retain most of their earnings. Companies can't do that in a day. They have to do that over a long period of time.

Like people, these companies go through rough periods. An analogy might be to think of a company as a person. If that were the case, and I were seeking a partner or possibly a mate, the three most important attributes I'd be looking for would be trustworthiness, truthfulness, and unselfishness. If I measure these qualities in terms of a day or an event, I'm going to be disappointed. People disappoint us all the time in the short term. Just because you messed up yesterday, why would anything change? Those characteristics are the fiber by which you govern your life. So if the people I trust possess those characteristics I identified, trustworthiness, truthfulness, and unselfishness, they most likely get back on track even if they messed up yesterday.

Think of kids for a moment. As they grow older, trying to figure out who they are and what kind of life they want, some get it right most of the time, and some get it wrong most of the time. In their hearts, they probably want to get everything right, and they might even have weeks like that. What inevitably takes place is that something that happened in the past pops up and hits them in the future, and they've got all these major problems connected to something they did a year ago or a month ago. It's hard to get yourself on track when that's your problem. The same is true of companies, so I don't buy companies like that. I already know what's going to happen, and I also know that if I do buy them, I'm going to have to keep dealing with problems. Because I choose companies for the reasons I mentioned, I know that when something pops up, they have a whole lot more energy to get things right.

I'm as careful about the companies I trust as I am the people I trust, and you should be too. Businesses are self-cleansing. Those that have high standards when they hire someone who, let's say, lies, cheats, and steals, will be very uncomfortable in that environment, and they will leave. But if you have lower standards, and someone who lies, cheats, and steals is in an environment where people don't tolerate that, they're going to leave. Let's say I have a really bad feeling about a company. Then someone else will tell me, "But Joe/Lisa is a good person." And I'll say, "But they're working there."

I'm being extreme here, but I don't care how Joe or Lisa rate on the good-person scale. By working for that company, they are measuring their own needs in a way that allows them to deflect and rationalize behaviors in their employers that they otherwise wouldn't accept. But they get a nice paycheck, so they deal with it, but they are part of the company. When I buy a company, that's what I'm looking for—those characteristics. I want a company that would drop a product that is questionable. When I see a company with a problem, and they say they'll improve, I say, "So what?" They're only going to get worse again. I'm looking for trends that are improving and a company that doesn't have to reestablish itself every six months.

Here's something I tell my clients. None of us gets to choose our children the way we can choose a stock. Children are our family; we live with them. We do what we must. But stocks are a choice. However, sometimes we treat our investments the way we do our families. We make poor decisions about them, we make excuses for them, and if we're not careful, the dysfunctional relationship can cost us money.

When I graduated from Wharton, my first job was assistant town manager in a Connecticut suburb. Before I reported for work, the town manager called to tell me there had been an election and the other party won. He explained he was sure he would be replaced, but he was not sure about me.

I asked myself, Why would I want to live my life with a career (job) that, no matter how well I performed, was to be determined by an election? I made a very quick decision and resigned before I showed for work.

It helped teach me to be careful not to personalize events in my life that had absolutely nothing to do with me. When things do not go your way, always remember it may have more to do with events beyond your control. While it does not exonerate us from being responsible, it helps make us understand a rude and mean person is just that—rude and mean. It has nothing to do with you or me. So don't personalize it.

Back to proactive instead of reactive. To be successful at investing, very little of the day-to-day action has anything to do with you. If you take it personally, you are very likely to take on the view that you're a victim. Never forget the market cares not at all about you or what you think.

For the past twenty-five years, I have driven about 250 miles one way every week. You see, much of the time I was working in Albany, NY, Philadelphia, PA, and Cape May, NJ, but each Friday I would be driving from those places to be with my wife and family.

Early on, I was becoming a madman driving. I told myself the only thing that could change was me and to stop thinking anyone was purposely cutting me off, etc. You see, I was personalizing behaviors by others I had convinced myself were directed at me.

When you personalize market actions, it means the market wins, and you are not in control! To be a successful investor, you must be in control!

PLAN FOR WEALTH, NOT MONEY

Money is something you spend. Wealth is something you accumulate. Money is momentary. Wealth is long term if properly managed.

As I already shared with you, when I was a young man, I knew that I wanted to be wealthy, but I wasn't in a rush. At the time, I was in my twenties, recently married, and starting a family. Still, even at that young age, I was willing to wait to become wealthy in my sixties, which seemed like a long time away. Why? Because I believed that if I followed textbook, data-driven investment strategies, they would make me wealthy. And they did.

At age twenty-two, I had nothing. At age thirty-two, I had $10,000. Today, I'm worth more than $50,000,000. I'm in the top one-tenth of the top 1 percent. But that journey required time and faith—time when I had to just turn off my brain and have faith in the process. This is one of the most important, nonnegotiable parts of my approach. You don't just invest your money; you invest your time. You also invest your faith.

Warren Buffett, Berkshire Hathaway CEO who, with a net worth of over $85 billion, is considered the fourth-wealthiest person in the world (behind Amazon founder Jeff Bezos, Microsoft cofounder Bill Gates, and the Bernard Arnault family, owner of LVMH), says that when he buys something, he buys it forever. He says that if you aren't willing to hold on to a stock for ten years, you shouldn't think for ten minutes about buying it. Wealth takes time, and as Buffett so succinctly puts it, "You can't produce a baby in one month by getting nine women pregnant."[13]

That approach—long-term investment strategies—has made me wealthy and can make you wealthy too. First, though, I need to clarify something.

When I tell people to think long term, they often think I'm talking about putting their money in savings accounts or bonds. But I'm not. I know why those sorts of investment strategies can seem attractive. It's because there's no volatility. When you lack volatility, you lack opportunity. Even at its worst, the stock market is still the best option.

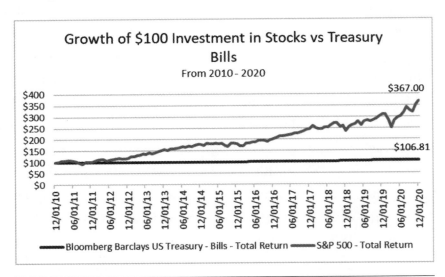

13   "Forbes World's Billionaires List: The Richest in 2021," Forbes, https://www. forbes.com/billionaires/

Volatility is a statistical measure of the dispersion of returns for a given security or market index. In most cases, the higher the volatility, the riskier the security. Volatility is often measured as either the standard deviation or variance between returns from that same security or market index. In the securities markets, volatility is often associated with big swings in either direction. For example, when the stock market rises and falls more than one percent over a sustained period of time, it is called a 'volatile' market. An asset's volatility is a key factor when pricing options contract.[14]

You've probably seen the advertisements where a popular credit card company asks, "What's in your wallet?" The car salesperson says, "Well, how much can you afford?" Every time you consider buying something, the person trying to sell you wants to know how much money you have.

What the credit card company is telling you is that you don't have to have anything in your wallet. They will loan it to you at 18 percent or more. What you need to have is their credit card. My message is the opposite, and my goal for you is to avoid that trap. Don't think about just what you have in your wallet, but what it takes to get it there—and what that amount of money will be worth down the road. Sure, you might be able to qualify for any number of expensive, maybe even life-changing purchases. But ask yourself if that money you're spending for a car, a swimming pool, or even a house could serve your better as an investment than it does consumed.

When I first started with Hayden Stone all those years ago, I was eager for knowledge. So I was surprised when I read the age and earnings of the average BMW buyer. This was in 1970. I remember looking at the demographics—how old the buyers were, how much

---

14   Adam Hayes, "Volatility," Investopedia, March 13, 2020, https://www. investopedia.com/terms/v/volatility.asp.

they earned—and it was then that I realized something that I had never before considered. It hit me like a bolt. I went home, my head still reeling, and told my wife, "The people who buy those cars can't afford them. If only the people who could really afford them bought them, the company would be out of business."

OVERNIGHT SUCCESS TAKES A WHILE

I didn't learn the value of sustainability overnight, although I did learn the value of planning. The most important thing my mother gave me was the belief that she presumed I would be successful. In her mind, that success was probably connected to money, and somehow she conveyed that belief to me. I didn't know what that meant to me at the time, but I accepted her version of my potential. When I was in ninth grade, I won the American Legion Award, not because I was the smartest kid in the city but because of an essay I wrote. I didn't think it was a big deal. I also ran for and lost a race for president of my junior high's student council, an experience that devastated me. One of the teachers who was genuinely interested in me tried to explain that I shouldn't take it personally because a lot of kids were intimidated by me. Looking back, it makes sense. Perhaps because of the path my mother's expectations put me on, I was already planning far beyond school, and I think that ability to visualize, plan, and look ahead has made me able to help others plan and succeed.

From a young age, I always had a ten-year plan. I knew if I put that plan in a drawer or another safe place, I'd never see it again, so I put it in my wallet. That way, I could know it was there and be reminded by its presence.

Many people don't succeed because they're too afraid of losing. People who succeed need to deal with, tolerate, and naturally embrace losing because it's part of winning. I know that when it comes to investing, but I'll confess that, after that early defeat, I decided I'd never run for anything again, and I never did. That might look like retreat, but for me it was a matter of where I decided to focus my attention and learn from my mistakes.

Early in my career I used to say I was great at foundations, but I could never sustain it. One day I looked at someone I knew very well who was more of a plodder. I looked at him and thought I did better than he did, but he was better at building on what he did. I decided to do what he was doing, which was *sustaining*. Once I realized I had to sustain daily what I was doing, I blew right past him.

Years later, once he retired, he visited my office and said something that surprised me. "Tom, if I could have done what you did, I'd still be working." He had decided to try to spin too many proverbial plates in the air. As happens in such situations, one sucked the energy out of the other. His two interests weren't compatible. In metaphorical terms, he wanted to have his cake and eat it too, but it ate him.

On the other hand, I had to learn sustainability, along with other rules. At first I wanted to be like everybody else. Today I don't want to be like anybody except me. I think we get there, most of us, at least. As you gain the investor's outlook, you also gain the personal outlook that helps you accept and sustain yourself just the way you are.

So here's the outlook that made me wealthy and can make you wealthy as well:

- Invest for the long term. That means you need discipline.

- Invest in the stock market.

- Once you plant those seeds, give them time to grow.

- Make wise purchasing decisions.

It sounds simple, doesn't it? That's because it is. What's not simple is the human brain. As I described earlier in this book, the marshmallow test showed that children have problems delaying gratification, even when they were told they'd receive double the reward. Double! That unwillingness to defer gratification doesn't change much when we grow up.

> **Remember, it's not what's in your wallet. It's what's *not* in your wallet, because it's wisely invested.**

Remember, it's not what's in your wallet. It's what's *not* in your wallet, because it's wisely invested.

Part of our anxiety about the stock market is that we won't be able to match or beat the market. Indexing—that is, investing in indices that summarize market activity—can work for a passive investor.

Because I am an active investor, I don't index, and I do target 10 percent growth. Even if you did index and you only saw 8 percent growth, that would still be a great deal more growth than most people see, including in their homes. (More about that shortly.)

I truly believe that if you are not born wealthy and you come from an average background, other than winning the lottery, other than being extremely lucky, it's a lifetime journey. And if you're so young you think you'll be too old to enjoy your money down the road, you're wrong.

THE STOCK MARKET: AN EXAMPLE

Let's suppose that when I was born in 1945, my parents had invested one hundred dollars for me. Let's also suppose that they didn't put it under the mattress (or in the freezer, as I've witnessed more than one person doing) and watched the value drop along with the dollar. No, they invested it. But in what? That's the key here, so let's take a look at how that money would have fared.

In a savings account: Today, that sum would have grown to less than $1,000. That's better than under the mattress or in the freezer, but it's not much for all those years.

In bonds: That investment would have earned less than $1,800.

In stocks: That $100 would have grown to $175,000.

And that is the beauty of time.

It's not about how much you earn; it's about how much you keep—and how much you can make it grow.

WHY SO MANY ATHLETES GO BROKE

You're probably aware of the 2009 *Sports Illustrated* study of former NFL and NBA players. The study found that after two years of retirement, 78 percent of NFL players were struggling financially or flat broke. After five years of retirement, 60 percent of NBA players were broke.[15]Mike Tyson is famous not just for his boxing championships but for managing to go through more money (about $300 million) than some countries' gross domestic product. So retirement isn't just about making a lot of money. It's how you think about money—your outlook.

I was invited to meet with a professional athlete who was earning $5 million a year. We agreed that his career would cover a relatively short period of his life and that he needed to plan now for how to support himself and his family for a retirement of more than forty years. "Considering how much you will need in your retirement, and considering how much you'll have after taxes," I told him, "you need to try living on $500,000 and invest the rest."

When I told him how much he needed to invest annually to give himself the kind of income he would require after sports, I got fired before I got hired. The athlete said there was no way he could live on $500,000 a year. He had too many expenses. If he has expenses now, what's going to happen to him when his income stops when he's still a young man? What happens if, like approximately 70 percent of his fellow athletes, he has to deal with the financial ramifications of divorce?[16]

---

15   Pablo S. Torre, "How (and Why) Athletes Go Broke," *Vault*, March 23, 2009, https://vault.si.com/vault/2009/03/23/how-and-why-athletes-go-broke.

16   Jay P. Granat, "Athletes and Divorce: Eleven Causes of Break Ups Among Athletes," HighNetWorthDivorces.com, https://www.highnet-worthdivorces.com/athletes-divorce-eleven-causes-break-ups-among-athletes/#:~:text=While%20the%20divorce%20rate%20among,that%20is%20approximately%20seventy%20percent.&text=There%20are%20eleven%20reasons%20that,athletes'%20marriages%20en.

I've encountered individuals in just about every high-earning profession who make life-changing mistakes when it comes to investing. They don't do it because they lack intelligence, and they certainly don't do it because they lack sufficient cash. They do it because they don't understand the concepts you are learning in this book. Regardless of how much you earn, you work for your money, and then your money works for you. Note that I didn't say, "You work for your money, you invest a little, double it, and then buy a Rolls-Royce." If cars are your thing, you can do that when you're closer to my age—if you still want to.

TIME IS MONEY

I can't think of a clearer way to put it, yet to many, it's a nontraditional way to look at both time and money.

Using the concept of the hypothetical penny we invested in 1776, I shortened the time period from birth to eighty-five years, thinking most people would identify eighty-five to be a reasonable lifetime. Here's how I broke it down. Suppose you invest $1,000?

At age eighty-five, if your investment earned 2 percent, you would have increased its value to $5,382.

Now let's suppose your investment earned 5 percent. That's a little better. When you reached age eighty-five, that $1,000 investment would have grown to $63,000.

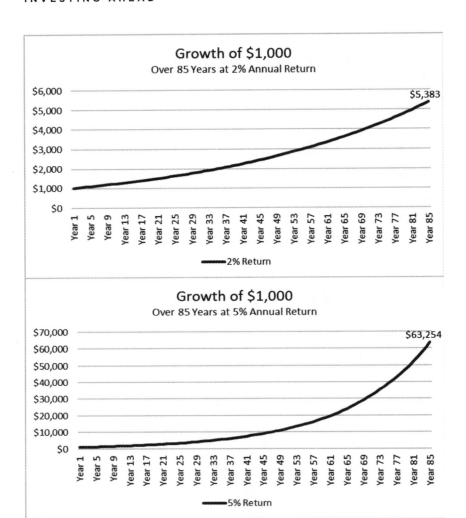

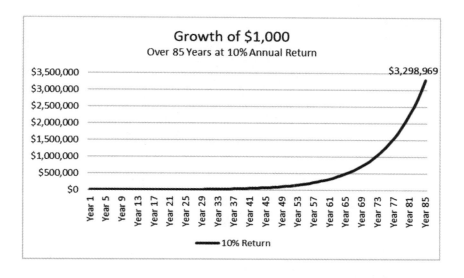

But now let's suppose you did what my clients and I have done over the years, and you enjoyed a return of 10 percent on your investment. That means you didn't touch your money; you simply left it where it was regardless of what was going on in the market or the economy. At age eighty-five, you would have turned that $1,000 into $3,298,000. In each of these cases, you started with the same amount of money. In each of these cases, you did not give into the need for instant gratification. You didn't pull that metaphorical plant out of the ground to look at its roots and see if it was producing yet. You simply went on with your life—maintaining the outlook that I advocate, and that is knowing the lure of *right now* is nothing compared to the wealth and security of the future. Picture that initial $1,000 compared to more than $3 million. Pretend you can choose between one and the other—because you can. Why would you want to limit that initial amount's ability to grow into a sum that can change your life?

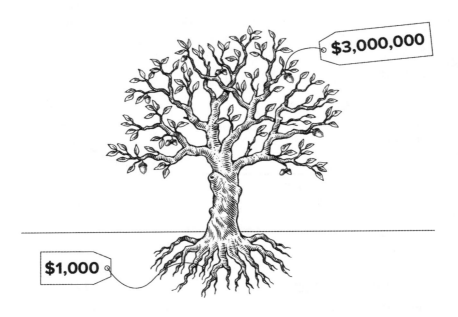

To most people, a million dollars is still a lot of money. So if somehow you earn, win, or inherit that much money, you're probably not going to think anything about spending a couple of hundred thousand when you don't realize what that's really worth. Instead, I think it's helpful to think in terms of how much wealth you would need to pay yourself a certain amount of money in retirement. For simplicity, let's say you want to be able to pay yourself $100,000. You would need about $2 million to $2.5 million. Therefore, when you look at $100,000, don't look at just that. Look at $2 million to $2.5 million because that's how much it's going to take you to produce that annual $100,000. So if you get $1 million, and you immediately spend $200,000 of it, you will need $4 million to produce $200,000—and now you've consumed $200,000 forever out of the principle.

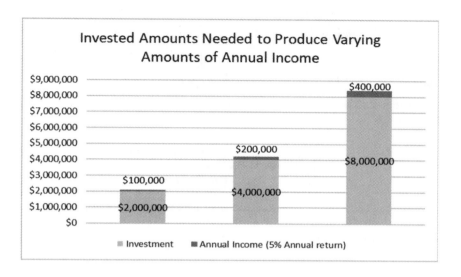

Let's look at another example. What if you invested $40,000 instead of spending $50,000 for a car? Keep the car you have, invest the $40,000, and use the extra $10,000 to either repair the car you have or as part of your emergency fund to handle the next crisis that demands your full financial attention. In addition to the money you spend daily, weekly, monthly, and annually, you should have that fund for emergencies as well as a much larger investment fund. That first money pool, the spending pool, should be only for meeting your obligations in the short term. The investment money pool should be for meeting your obligations in the long term.

Suppose you want to buy a Rolls-Royce? It has a $400,000 price tag, but you can swing it. It's not as simple as it looks, because it's really not about the asking price for the car. You need to work backward from that. Ultimately, you need $8 million to buy that Rolls-Royce because that's what you need to produce a cash flow. That's what many people don't understand. They understand only the present value, what that money will buy today. I do own a Rolls, but I was almost seventy when I purchased it, and the cost was about 1 percent of my net worth.

Too many people have a current, right-this-minute approach to investing. Do it now. Make a bunch. Get out before it crashes. That's not how investing works for those of us interested in long-term wealth. You have to be able to afford one or two bad quarters. Would you rather lose for sure instead of win with a high degree of certainty over the long run?

THE CONSUMER'S OUTLOOK: THE TOXIC TEN EXCUSES

- I can afford the payments.

- I deserve it.

- Can't wait until I get my tax refund.

- I'm approved for a lot more.

- I'll have this paid off in no time.

- This deal's too good to pass up.

- Everybody else has one.

- I have to have it.

- I'm going to splurge.

- You only live once.

Let's look at these toxic ten excuses for a moment.

The consumer outlook convinces you that you can afford the payments. The investment outlook would say great—instead of making payments with or without interest, let's invest that money.

The same with a tax refund. And furthermore, if you are an efficient tax planner, you should not be getting much of a "refund" for your interest-free loan to the government.

I'm sure you deserve it, whatever it is, but more than that, you deserve a secure future. If you're approved for a lot more than whatever loan or credit card you're being offered, that's probably because you're credit worthy, and you can stay that way by not acquiring needless debt. Instead of congratulating yourself on how soon you'll be able to pay off a debt, ask yourself how much of that money you can afford to invest for the long term.

If you think a deal is too good to pass up, remind yourself of every other deal you ever felt that way about and ask yourself if you were right. What would happen if you did pass up this deal? How would your life change? And again—what would happen if you took that money you're willing to part with in this too-good deal and put it toward your future wealth instead of your current craving?

"Everyone else has one" is a weak excuse to justify something you're convinced will make you feel better about yourself. Long-term wealth and security will make you feel much better.

"I have to have it." Why? What need are you trying to fill? How many times have you tried to fill that need with other purchases? You want that current prize now because you don't want to take the time to consider the wisdom of your decision.

Telling yourself you're splurging is another excuse to distract yourself from the fact that this is the way you always operate when dealing with money. But go ahead. Call it splurging. Claim you're letting go of money you should be holding on to because you only live once. Then think about it. What would happen if you didn't splurge on that trip, that car, or that case of Napa Valley wine? Would your life really be that unhappy? Compare the momentary satisfaction of that indulgence to watching your money grow over the years and knowing that it was because you *didn't* give in to a momentary urge to spend it.

The consumer's outlook seeks immediate gratification. It seeks escape, perhaps in the literal sense of a vacation or in the acquiring of perceived image-building toys, clothing, vehicles, or real estate. Each purchase stimulates the pleasure center in the brain. Yes, just like drugs, alcohol, or food, spending money can activate a region of your brain with dopamine receptors. Dopamine, a neurotransmitter, helps control the brain's reward and pleasure centers. Researchers at Stanford found that even seeing pictures of items you'd like to buy activates that region of the brain.[17] But here's the thing about instant gratification. The brain likes to feel pleasure, the more, the better. Once the thrill wears off, the more likely your brain is to crave that same pleasure again. The consumer's outlook appetite is voracious and its satisfaction momentary. The investor's outlook isn't about right now; it's about the future.

Everyone, including you, has the potential to have more wealth than they ever dreamed of if they have the investor's and not the consumer's outlook. And the good news is that once you are aware of which outlook you possess, you can change from consumer to investor.

EVEN IF YOU FAIL, YOU SUCCEED

Any time you start investing is the right time. Of course, it's better to start young, but regardless of when you do, you and your family will benefit much more than if you pass altogether on the opportunity.

For example, $1,000 invested at age forty-five, earning 10 percent overall, will be worth $45,259 at age eighty-five. At that age, to achieve the $3.2 million that eighty-five years produces would

---

17   NeuroTrackerX Team, "Why Shopping Makes You Feel High," NeuroTracker, Dec. 18, 2016, https://www.neurotrackerx.com/post/shopping-makes-feel-high.

require an investment of $72,000. At 2 percent, that money would earn $158,000. For most people, a sum invested at age forty-five would be used long before age eighty-five for retirement needs.

If you don't get 10 percent, you're still going to be just fine. Let's just say you're terrible and you're 20 percent worse than the averages. As a result, instead of doubling your money every seven years, you will double it every nine years, and that is still significant. Ultimately, if you have proper goals and you fail, you still succeed.

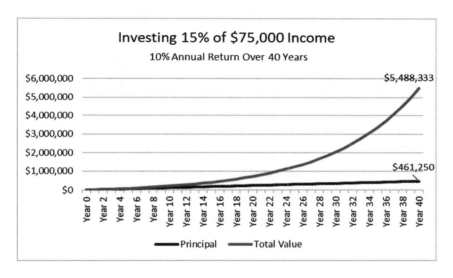

That's what I used to tell myself. I would think something like this: *even if I do a lousy job at this, even if I don't get what I should get, maybe only 8 percent or 7 percent, it's still going to be a heck of a lot more than I'll get being fearful and doing little or nothing.* As long as you have that perspective, you are going to be successful. If I had all my money in stocks over my lifetime, I'd be worth a lot more than I am.

Whenever you buy something, you should have some idea of what the historical long-term rates of return are. When you do that in stocks, you can rest assured, as we've just discussed, that it's around 10 percent—over time. With real estate, it's going to be 2 percent to

4 percent. With cash, you can be sure that it's going to be somewhere around 1 percent and 4 percent.

When my grandson was born, I invested $25,000 for him. That pot of money could grow to $82,240,000, but the possibility is nil because it will be spent for something like college and taxes, which could reduce the return. Still, the numbers are amazing when you consider that the grandson would not have to do anything to earn it except wait.

You don't have to be a history buff—especially not in these uncertain, anxiety-provoking times—to understand how politics and world events can reduce the value of a dollar. Yet all the negative events in our history didn't result in that penny I mentioned earlier turning into millions.

Sound investing is not like an ATM or a slot machine. It's not like a savings account. Over the years, you won't always like the numbers you see, and a momentary loss can hurt. At the moment you can tell yourself, "This is the worst it's ever been. Something is really wrong, and I have to do something." But remember that the toe you stub today always hurts worse than the toe you stubbed a year ago, so when you stub your toe financially, you can't react and start yanking out money just because you're in pain. You have to know you aren't going to be limping indefinitely.

At times like those, you need to remind yourself that investing for the future requires absolute commitment. Ben Franklin supposedly said, "A penny saved is a penny earned." I say, "supposedly" because all kinds of quotes have been attributed to poor Ben. However, if he actually is the source of this quote, he was wrong. A penny invested is much, much more than a penny earned.

IF WE WERE SQUIRRELS, WE'D BE DEAD

If you were a squirrel, you would have a seasonal approach to life, and that approach would be getting through the winter. Wall Street is short term. Life is long. We have to think about where we need to be throughout our lives and how to get through all those winters.

As investors, we need to start storing up for the future. Wise investing is about where we are today and how much time we have to start using what we've stored. As we've already discussed, the need to consume gets in the way. If we were a squirrel,

Wise investing is about where we are today and how much time we have to start using what we've stored.

we would be well dressed, live in the nicest nests, gorge ourselves all summer, and come winter, we would be dead.

Many beginning investors cash out when they see their first double. Then they start consuming—probably because they always had the consumer's outlook. Cashing out in those circumstances is a mistake, but it's one many frequently make—because of the greed I mentioned earlier.

As I share frequently with my clients, you need to know that opportunity is all around you, and the biggest opportunity is the wealth that comes with time. Most people don't hear that opportunity knocking because they are distracted by what they want right now.

I'm not trying to say squirrels are smarter than we are. After all, they are motivated by survival to store those nuts. Nor am I trying to say you are a financial failure if you've taken money you could have invested and spent it on something that won't produce wealth for you. I am, however, trying to help you see the opportunities

73

you have—right now—to change your mindset and your outlook about money.

For instance, have you ever had to clean out your garage, tool shed, or extra bedroom? You might have even said to yourself, "Look at all this junk!"

There's that trailer, all the tools you don't use, the out-of-date computers and televisions, the exercise equipment that have become hangers for the clothes you don't have room for in the closet and haven't worn for years. Don't even get me started about the sporting goods that seemed like such great ideas at the time you bought them. We all have junk, and when you look around at yours, I want you to realize this. Everything you see around you used to be money! Now think about the penny I mentioned earlier. If you had invested the money you spent for at least some of what you now think of as junk, imagine how that money could grow and become wealth.

Ask yourself how much more you could have invested. How much less could you have consumed? Could you have been satisfied with a slightly smaller car or a slightly smaller home? Now consider all you spent and what it bought for you. How much of it would you buy again? Stay with this outlook, and let it direct you the next time you consider making a purchase. With the outlook of the savvy investor, you will find decision-making much easier than it was before, and with that extra money, you'll be able to start seriously investing. Honestly, though, it's more about the outlook and the mindset than the money, especially at first. The outlook and the mindset will enable you to invest wisely and for the long term, whatever your age, starting now.

HOW TO MAKE MY APPROACH WORK FOR YOU

- Plan for wealth, not money.

- Invest in the stock market.

- Invest for the long term.

- Buy like Warren Buffett—forever.

- Learn to tolerate volatility.

- Know that athletes and other wealthy people go broke because they can't imagine and adhere to simple rules of investing.

- Remember that today's financial pain is like the toe you just stubbed versus the one you stubbed last year; it just feels worse.

- Don't cash out.

- Learn the toxic ten of a consumer's outlook.

- When you start matters, but regardless of when you do it, just start.

- Develop an investor's outlook about how much you spend.

Now that you have an investor's outlook and you're determined to curb your spending, maybe you're thinking of investing in a newer, larger—translated, more expensive—home. Before you do, please take a look at the next chapter.

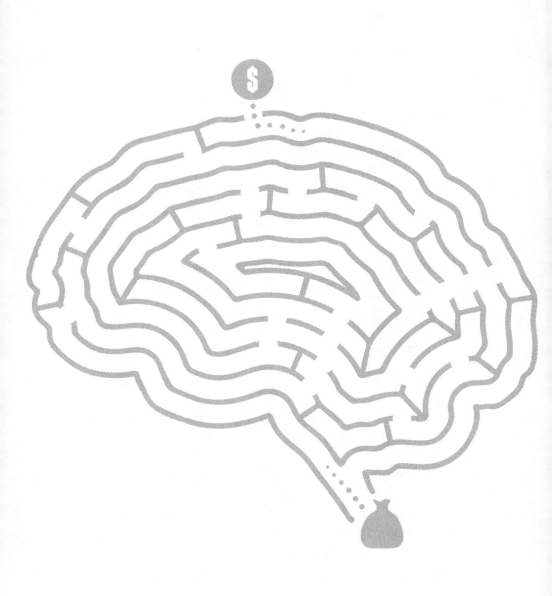

CHAPTER FOUR

YOUR HOME: GREATEST INVESTMENT OR GREATEST EXPENSE?

Curranism #4: *"The term 'house poor'*
exists for a reason."

Earlier, we saw that traditional long-term investments in bonds and savings accounts won't actually create wealth. There's one other traditional long-term investment strategy to beware of, and that is real estate. But isn't owning a home the American Dream? Absolutely. The misconception here is that owning a home is a good investment.

When I started in the financial services business, a residence was never considered part of an investment plan. It was never part of someone's financial picture because we understood that it was not a good investment. It was really a place, a residence, the house where you lived. In addition to that, the rate of return on residential real estate is only 2 to 5 percent, and that's based on records going back to 1900. The problem is that people have this misconception that their residence is a great investment. It may be a good investment depending on how you look at it, but it's not a *great* investment.

Still, many embrace the fallacy that by the time they get to retirement, their dwelling will have contributed significantly to their net worth. Not at 2 to 5 percent, it won't! On top of that, home-ownership involves yearly, even monthly expenses—money out of your pocket. The return you're dealing with is a negative return. The home is a cost, not a net contributor to long-term wealth. Owning a home takes money out of your pocket for property taxes, mainte-nance, and insurance.

A 2019 Bankrate survey found that 63 percent of millennial homeowners expressed regrets about their current home purchase, the highest share of any generation. Forty-four percent of homeown-ers said they had regrets about their home purchase. Their top regret? Unexpected maintenance or hidden costs, according to the survey.[18]

For these and other reasons, I sometimes say purchasing a home creates financial *insecurity*. Over the years, I've had many conver-sations with people who have been mistaking home buying for investing. That can be a tough conversation because for some people, their house is almost as sacred as their children. But it's a conversa-tion we need to have. After taxes and expenses, a house will consume 40 percent to 50 percent of your disposable income. Plus, do not forget how much time you spend in "sweat labor." That can leave

---

18   Deborah Kearns. "Homebuyers' top regrets," Bankrate, Feb. 2019.

you stretched thin with no cash to invest. Think about it like this. You're pouring most of your extra money into the place you live, a place that is growing older right along with you. You are spending money for taxes and repairs, maybe additions to the house, and because you're doing that, you don't have enough money left over to invest in something that will grow to an average of 10 percent when you retire. It's a case of robbing Peter to pay Paul, only in this case you're robbing your future financial security. You simply can put all your resources into your home and ignore the investments that will truly pay off for you. Here's a personal example.

In 1950, my parents moved from Philadelphia and bought a $9,999 bungalow in suburbia. They spent their lives there. My mother passed away, and about five years later, in 2001, my father decided to move into senior housing and asked me to sell the house for him. I then sold it for $115,000. In order to meet the requirement for an FHA loan, we had to make some improvements and make some changes, so we ended up with $110,000. At first glance—when you think from ten to one hundred plus, that seems like a huge rate of return, doesn't it? I did the valuation on it again using the 2 to 5 percent rate of return, and it came out to about 3.5 percent.

Over the years, my mother and father had added a third bedroom, finished the basement, and made all the improvements one has to make after all that time in the same home. When I did the valuation, I was not surprised to discover a return of 3.5 percent. And that's from 1950 to 2001. The reason I wasn't surprised is because that's about average; even today when the cost of improvements is factored in, the return falls to less than 2 percent. I wouldn't be shocked if you told me you were thinking of your family home as part of your retirement income; it's certainly worth more than you might earn from a lot of your investments. However, the truth is that despite your investment in its upkeep, the home you may be considering a long-term investment won't have a much better rate of return than the money in your savings account.

That's not how we think about money we spend on a home, though, and it's not the way we think about money in general. When most people discuss their money, they say, "We can spend it here, or we can spend it there," and the problem is that the keyword has always been *spend*. There's not enough emphasis on how they're going to invest the money. Spending a lot on a residence gives us the impression that we're really investing. Others, ranging from the people selling you the house to the flooring contractor who's giving you an estimate on what your "investment" in hardwood will cost, are happy to continue that false impression and might actually believe it themselves. No one feels guilty. However, if we were to look at it in a sound, financial way, we would say, "Wow. That really is costing me."

Instead, when considering a purchase, we look at the schools or look at the neighborhood. Even though all those things could be perfect, there's still a cost to it. That house is an expense. It's not going to provide the rate of return of other investments. Yet we perpetuate the myth.

People tell themselves real estate is a good investment because they don't want to feel guilty. That big purchase satisfies a wish and a want, and after a while, many just believe the investment myth, even if it makes no sense and even if there's proof to the contrary.

I'm not telling you that you shouldn't own a home. I'm just pointing out that you shouldn't buy one because you think it's a wise investment. Nor should you think homeownership is a wise investment because a home's value appreciates. As I just showed you with my parents' home, the appreciation looked significant, but the rate of return was anything but. Here's what you should add in:

- insurance

- utilities

- real estate taxes

- roof repairs

- flooring

- additions

- and, if you stay there long enough, probably eventual and costly remodeling in kitchens and bathrooms

Can you see how the cost of this "investment" can add up?

The biggest chunk of the average American's budget goes toward housing, which accounts for about 37 percent of take-home pay. Many people spend even more.[19] The standard measure of housing affordability is 30 percent or less of pretax income, and it's been in place for more than eighty years since the United States Housing Act of 1937 was passed, establishing public housing assistance for low-income families. Still, Harvard researchers found that in total, between renters and owners, nearly 39 million American households, that is, 33 percent, are paying more than they can afford for their homes.[20]Many people bought homes at the top of the real estate market, and after the market collapse, many had to sell those homes because they had borrowed against their homes, their payments had ballooned, or they were otherwise upside down on their loans. In many cases, the values of those homes had dropped, and the owners could not sell them for what

---

19   Lauren Lyons Cole. "Forget coffee and avocado toast—most people blow nearly 40% of their money in the same place," *Business Insider*, August 24, 2017.

20   Lauren Lyons Cole and Andy Kiersz, "Harvard researchers say one-third of Americans overpay for housing—and renters have it the worst," *Business Insider*, June 17, 2017.

they owed on them, let alone for more. Their needs and finances, not sound investing wisdom, dictated when they bought and sold. That's because your house is where you live; it's not a true investment.

Besides, what happens if you do sell your house and make some money? Where are you going to live? Most people buy another house, and the whole process starts again.

WHAT'S GOING TO BE DIFFERENT THIS TIME?

In 2008, I did a presentation about the history of residential housing prices. I showed real estate prices based on US government data from 1900. The numbers went along at the 2 to 5 percent rate of return. And then in the period just prior to the Great Depression, real estate had this tremendous spike, almost straight up. And then, of course, we had the crash. After that, real estate was going along at that 2 to 4 percent period again until we got into the post 9/11 period in the 2000s. And then real estate spiked up again.

After explaining that, I said to the audience, "What do these two periods show you? Why would we think the second spike would be different than the first one?" Those spikes were not sustainable.

And of course, the second spike wasn't different from the first one, but that doesn't keep people from getting caught up in their emotions. When we have these spikes prior to a stock market crash, people flock to real estate in tremendous numbers. If they had one house, they now have two houses. If they already owned two houses, they now have four houses.

Instead of reacting, you have to be able to look at those long-term rates of return. If you bought into one of those spikes, you'd have to ask yourself, What is it that you think is going to be different this time?

HOW TO BUY A HOUSE

I'm not against owning a home. I own four of my own, but I didn't start out that way, and I didn't view those homes as investments. When my wife and I bought our first home, our peers were buying their homes for about $60,000. This was the 1960s, remember, and you could buy a lot of house for that money. We bought our first house for $20,000. We spent less than we could have because we wanted that extra money to go not to the place we lived but to our long-term investments.

People understand absolutes, but they don't understand the rate of return. The basic definition is the profit or loss you make on an investment in terms of a yearly percentage. The rate of return is the ratio of your income from an investment over the cost, including hidden costs, of that investment. My definition is really a question. If you're going somewhere that takes three and a half hours driving—and you're going to walk, why bother? Stay at home. Many people have a false conception of what they're going to achieve when they buy a home. If you recognize that it's 2 percent to 4 percent, why consider it an investment when it's going to be that much hassle? Why not just buy a bond? Do you suppose, as I suggested earlier, it's because we're trying to justify our actions?

It takes time. It takes discipline. It takes work. But it will get you where you want to be.

There is a better way. It takes time. It takes discipline. It takes work. But it will get you where you want to be. You don't have to take those chances. Just do what's right. Most of us know what that is, and we know when we're bending the rules a little bit. We know what we should do, but we don't always, and I think most people would recognize that they spend too much for housing; they just don't feel trapped by it. Regardless of how you feel, numbers don't lie. You don't have to invest as much in a home as you've been led to do, and you certainly shouldn't convince yourself that something is a good investment just because you want it.

THE GREATEST INVESTMENT MYTH

We want the house, but as I pointed out earlier, we don't want to feel guilty about putting out all that money. So we tell ourselves it's a great investment. After all, it has a pool, a sunken tub, antique lighting features, hardwood floors. None of those will be worth anything if the house is in a declining neighborhood. Don't look at the surface benefits. Buy the junk house, tear it down, and improve the land. I never realized the huge premiums developers get for doing just that.

I would put something up for sale, and a developer would come in and say, "This is what I'll pay."

Then I started thinking, and I asked myself, "Well, I wonder what he'll get." That's a natural question that anyone would consider. Then I wondered what would happen if I sold the property to the developer. He would develop it, and then when he sold it, what would the cost be? And finally, of course, I asked myself, "What would the cost be if I keep the land?" And that's what I did. I kept the land value at the price the developer was willing to pay me, checked with some general contractors to see what it would cost me to develop it. Then I had an idea of what I could get for it.

On some beachfront property, I paid $3 million for the land alone, which was obviously a big price. The cost of construction was about $1.5 million. The sales price was over $6 million. Why don't other people do that? For one, they don't want to be bothered. Going through all those steps is a lot of work, and when you work as your own developer, you're dealing with an unknown. There's tremendous risk, and that risk premium is a lot of money—probably 30 percent or so.

So why did I do it? Because I like diversification. I don't want to depend on any one thing to build my wealth. There were times I took all the risks, took on all the work, and didn't make any money. Should you do it? As everything I'm sharing with you in this book, that depends on you. Still, investing wisely in stocks, as I have done—and letting your interest compound—is the best investment you can make over time.

But those who insist on residential real estate being a key component to building wealth must leverage the home purchase with a big mortgage, and now the appreciation rate exceeds their mortgage interest.

FLIPPING OR SLIPPING?

You've seen them on TV, and so have I. Let's call them flippers.

Purchase a home, make a few easy and inexpensive changes, and there you are, ready to flip it—translated, make a lot of money for a minimal investment. I wish life worked this way. If it did, I'd be flipping a lot of homes and investing much less in stocks. Apparently, a lot of people believe it though.

ATTOM Data Solutions, curator of the nation's premier property database and first property data provider of data as a service, in its first-quarter 2020 *US Home Flipping Report*, showed that 53,705 single-family homes and condominiums in the United States were flipped in the first quarter. That number represents 7.5 percent of all home sales in the country during the quarter and is up from 6.3 percent in the fourth quarter of 2019 and from 7.3 percent in the first quarter of 2019, to the highest level since the second quarter of 2006. The gross profit on the typical home flip nationwide (the difference between the median sales price and the median paid by investors) also increased in the first quarter of 2020, to $62,300. That was up slightly from $62,000 in the fourth quarter of 2019 and from $60,675 in the first quarter of last year. But with home prices rising, the typical gross flipping profit of $62,300 translated into only a 36.7 percent return on investment compared to the original acquisition price.[21] A 36.7 percent return seems like a big number. But out of that gross profit comes the added cost of improvements and closing costs plus commissions to sell.

There are two primary approaches to flipping a property:

Repair and update. With this approach, you buy a property that you think will increase in value with certain repairs and updates. Ideally, you complete the work as quickly as possible and then sell at a price that exceeds your total investment (including the renovations).

Hold and resell. This type of flipping works differently. Instead of buying a property and fixing it up, you buy in a rapidly rising market, hold for a few months, and then sell at a profit.

Curb appeal goes just so far, and that was the case even when property was (relatively) easy to acquire. I can count off the problems, ranging from delays, to government regulations you thought you understood but really didn't, to theft, to incompetent or dishonest repair people, to the most important problem of all—unanticipated expenses. Then there are building permits, contractor delays, material delays, permit delays, and renovations and materials you had not budgeted for.

You'll find them everywhere.

Have you considered how much physical labor will be involved in this flip of yours? The 2019 *Cost vs. Value* report from *Remodeling* says the highest return on investment (ROI) is the following: new garage

---

21   "US Home Flipping Rate Increases to 14-Year High in First Quarter of 2020 While Returns Slump to Nine-Year Low," ATTOM, June 11, 2020.

door; stone veneer siding; wood decks; new windows; steel entry door. According to the report, you can recoup the cost of a new garage door by 97.5 percent.[22] Look at the following, and before you think about how much you will recoup, think about how much of your own money you will have to come up with before you make anything.

HOUSE VS. VALUE

- Garage door replacement, 97.5 percent

- Manufactured stone veneer, 94.9 percent

- Minor kitchen remodel, 80.5 percent

- Deck addition, wood, 75.6 percent

- Siding replacement, 75.6 percent

- Entry door replacement, steel, 74.9 percent

- Entry door replacement, vinyl, 73.4 percent

- Grand entrance, fiberglass, 71.9 percent

- Window replacement, wood, 70.8 percent

- Deck addition, composite, 69.1 percent

- Roofing replacement, asphalt shingles, 68.2 percent

- Bath remodel, midrange, 67.2 percent

- Major kitchen remodel, midrange, 62.1 percent

---

22   2019 Cost Vs. Value Report, Remodeling.

The list continues shrinking in value, all the way to a backyard patio with a return on investment of 55.2 percent and an upscale master suite addition with a return on investment of 50.4 percent.

Have you checked out the home's heating system? When was it installed, and how long can you expect it to survive? If the heating system was completely replaced, what about the furnace's blower fan? Was it running while workers were doing their drywall sanding, and is the interior of the furnace completely covered in drywall dust?

Labor is expensive. If you hire out all the labor you'll need on your investment house, how much will you have left for profit? Suppose you find out you need to rewire the house? Or you find hidden mold behind the shower? What about taxes? Will you be charged a short-term capital gains rate if you sell in less than a year, as you're surely hoping to?

Then, after you pay for all that labor, you have to put your property on the market. The more you wait, the longer you get to pay the mortgage, not to mention all the repairs you're probably still paying for. By now you have the idea, and I don't need to remind you of the stress involved with such gambles.

Let me just say flipping houses is a risky way to make a living. You're walking into a black hole of unknown expenses. You're also walking into something that requires a major investment of your time (which you could be using to make more reliable investments), and because of those risks, flipping can bring you a great deal of stress and anxiety before you earn a dime.

Suppose the flippers or the developers, in order to compete, wind up having to pay more and more for what they're going to sell the property for at the end of this cycle? Now they're looking at properties where, when I put my numbers to it, say, "If I do this, and I sell, I'm going to lose money." Why would I do that? I don't, but if that's your business, if that's how you need to earn your living, somehow you will convince yourself to do it anyway, on the hope that you will be able to sell it. And that's a great example of the greater fool theory, which says, in essence, "Surely there's someone out there who makes even worse financial decisions than I do."

THE GREATER FOOL THEORY

Actually, this theory is as much about hope as it is about fools. It suggests that there will always be an investor who will foolishly pay a higher price than the intrinsic worth of a security.

In a perfect greater fool situation, an investor will purchase questionably priced assets without any regard to their quality. If the theory holds, the investor will still be able to quickly sell them off to another greater fool, who could also be hoping to sell them quickly. It's kind of like that childhood game of musical chairs, where there was one fewer chair than kids. The music stopped, and all the kids grabbed a chair, leaving one unfortunate standing. What really drives the greater fool approach is its focus not on the value of a security but on finding someone willing to pay too much for it. The process continues until the most foolish of all these investors is the last one standing.

Eventually, speculative bubbles burst, and that leads to a rapid depreciation in prices. The theory also breaks down in other circumstances, including economic recessions and depressions. In 2008, when investors purchased faulty mortgage-backed securities, they had difficulty finding buyers when the market collapsed. One of the reasons was that these securities were built on debt that was of very poor quality.

By 2004, US homeownership had peaked at 70 percent. In late 2005, home prices started to fall, leading to a 40 percent decline in the

US Home Construction Index in 2006. Many subprime borrowers were no longer able to withstand high interest rates and began to default on their loans. Financial firms and hedge funds that owned in excess of $1 trillion in securities backed by these failing subprime mortgages also began to move into distress.[23]

As I've said before, investing is not gambling, and if you remember that—and if you work with a trusted advisor—you'll be less likely to become the greater fool theory's next victim.

Do not blindly follow the herd, paying higher and higher prices for something without any good reason.

Do your research and follow a plan.

Adopt a long-term strategy for investments to avoid bubbles.

Diversify your portfolio.

Control your greed, and resist the temptation to try to make big money within a short period of time.

Understand that there is no sure thing in the market, not even continual price inflation.[24]

---

23   James Chen, "Greater Fool Theory," Investopedia, Sept. 11, 2019.

24   "What Is the Greater Fool Theory?" Corporate Finance Institute.

AND IF YOU STILL WANT TO FLIP

Look at that house in that (relatively) OK neighborhood. Consider how much you might need to invest to flip it fast and make money like the flippers you've seen on television. Then think twice before you do it. Focus on investing in stocks. That's how you turn $10,000 into $50,000,000.

WHAT YOU NEED TO KNOW ABOUT INVESTING IN REAL ESTATE

The 70 percent rule states that an investor should pay no more than 70 percent of the after-repair value (ARV) of a property minus the repairs needed. The ARV is what a home is worth after it is fully repaired.

Here's an example: if a home's ARV is $150,000, and it needs $25,000 in repairs, then the 70 percent rule means that an investor should pay no more than $80,000 for the home: $150,000 x 0.70 = $105,000 − $25,000 = $80,000.[25]

YOU, THE LANDLORD

I've known people who were convinced they'd make more money renting out a home than using the money tied up in the home for investing. If you are thinking that way, you again need to think of your biggest commodity, and that is your time. If you've ever rented yourself, you know all the things that can go wrong that makes a renter have to call the landlord. Toilets. Sinks. Garbage disposals. Air

---

25 James McWhinney, "5 Mistakes That Can Make House Flipping A Flop," Investopedia, May 8, 2020, https://www.investopedia.com/articles/mort-gages-real-estate/08/house-flip.asp.

conditioners. No wonder most landlords who own more than one property do their own repairs.[26]

If you decide to hire a property-management firm to take care of maintenance issues, you'll have more time to concentrate on other matters, but you'll also be eating away at your profits. That's assuming you have profits after you deal with pest control, property taxes, landscaping expenses, and landlord insurance. While you're struggling to stay ahead of all these, you should also be stashing about 10 percent to 20 percent of your rental income for emergencies like roof damage and burst pipes.

Landlords make money two ways: renting at a price that covers their investment and doesn't leave money on the table, and by selling the property after it appreciates. That is, if it appreciates. There are lots of *ifs* when dealing with real estate, and that's because it isn't flexible. Once you own a piece of land, you cannot change where it is; you are stuck with the location until you sell.

> **There are lots of *ifs* when dealing with real estate, and that's because it isn't flexible.**

Between the years of 1963 to 2007, with very few exceptions, the average sale price of homes in the United States continued to increase. Surprisingly, house prices have increased rapidly more recently. The coronavirus seems to have boosted housing prices.

This brings us back to the real point of this chapter. A home is the place you live, the place where you can be with your family and get away from the demands of the outside world. I love my home, and I want you to enjoy yours.

---

26   "Real Estate Investing Guide," Investopedia, https://www.investopedia.com/articles/investing/090815/buying-your-first-investment-property-top-10-tips.asp

THE REALITIES OF REAL ESTATE

- After taxes and expenses, a house may consume 40–50 percent of your disposable income, which may leave you little left over to invest.

- Just because a home appreciates doesn't mean homeownership is a wise investment.

- No bells and whistles on a home will be worth anything if the house is in a declining neighborhood.

- Flipping houses is a risky way to make a living.

- Don't fall for the greater fool theory.

- Once you own a piece of land, you cannot change where it is; you are stuck with the location until you sell.

Next let's look at the way my clients and I have made money consistently over the years, a way that requires some simple steps and a lot of patience.

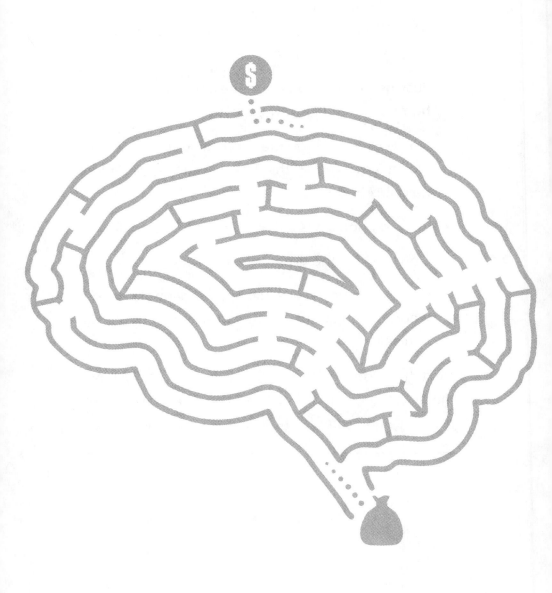

CHAPTER FIVE

CONSUME OR COMPOUND

Curranism #5: *"Committed long-term investors know that growth in stocks is like adolescent growth spurts. You know they are coming, but you cannot pinpoint the actual timing."*

S o I've warned you about Wall Street, and now I'm encouraging you to invest in stocks? Correct. That's the best way to make the kind of money I have with even a minimal investment and major self-control. It's the way I've made most of my money, and it's the way I've helped my clients make the most of theirs.

Think of investing in the stock market as your business, one unlike any other business, that will benefit from benign neglect. To run a business on a daily basis, you have to deal with problems, you have to be proactive, and that's what gets people in trouble when they're investing. You always need to know when to push and when to back off. With stocks, however, you really should back off all the time. Just buy good companies, invest in them for the long term, and back away.

Not everyone possesses the talents necessary to manage and run a business. But almost everyone—you included—can be a successful investor *if* they—and you—understand the power of compound interest and the time it requires to bear fruit.

But bear fruit it does. Let's suppose someone invests $7,500 in 1981 and chooses to compound. Thirty-six years later, that money would have grown to $231,845. It would have had its ups and downs, but it would have made its way to that $231,845. Adjusted for inflation, $7,500 would be worth $22,332.62 today.[27] You could have purchased any number of things with that money, but you would be hard pressed to make it grow to that amount.

GROWTH COMES IN SPURTS

Warren Buffett describes the stock market as "a device for transferring money from the impatient to the patient." After years in this business, I can tell you he's right.

If you've ever raised a child, you know that growth doesn't come in easy-to-predict increments. You know, as adolescence arrives, that growth surely will happen; you just don't know when. And then one day you blink your eyes, and they've grown three or four inches. It's not linear, and when you look back, you can see that your child's growth came in spurts. The same is true of the stock market. It grows in spurts, and sometimes something unpredictable happens, and it doesn't grow at all.

When you're looking at numbers like 1 percent, 2 percent, 3 percent, 4 percent, 5 percent, and 6 percent compounded, you can extract and extrapolate; you can calculate those numbers. But once

---

27 "Inflation Calculator," DollarTimes, https://www.dollartimes.com/inflation/.

you get to the higher numbers, they're not linear any longer. In 2019, for example, the stock market was up over 30 percent. But that's how you get to that average of 10 percent. It might be 30 percent; it might be zero this year, and that still is 15 percent over a two-year period. And then it might be 10 percent. We call it volatility. There's growth, ultimately, and you know it's coming. You just don't know when.

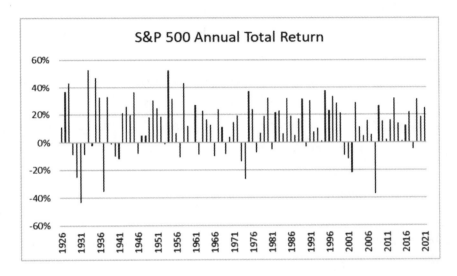

This doesn't frighten me, but of course, it concerns me. I'm a husband, a father, and a grandfather. I'm also what I hope is the voice of reason for the clients who put their faith and their futures into our firm. Long ago, in that first postcollege job of mine, I learned that I didn't want to be a salesperson. I wanted to be an advisor and a protector.

It seems to me that lack of patience in waiting for the win is what gets people into trouble. They don't wait.

The year I wrote most of this book (2019 and early 2020), the stock market was up more than 30 percent. That's how you get to the average of 10 percent—volatility—ups and downs. Many people have a good year like that one, and they end up selling because they think those gains can't be sustained. They *can't* be sustained—that's true—but that lack of sustainability is no reason to sell. For many years, I've watched people get in trouble when they let impatience and the refusal to wait take over their self-discipline. I sincerely hope I've talked some of them off the proverbial ledge. However, ultimately, we make our own decisions, right or wrong.

Also in 2020, as I was finishing this book, COVID-19 hit, and the stock market reflected the uncertainty in the country and in the world. At the time, my wife Peggy and I were at our home in Bermuda, where we had no choice but to stay for several months until we could get a flight out. I spent my days and many of my nights coordinating the transition of my Albany, New York, office to remote and talking to clients, telling them in essence that this, too, would pass.

You can imagine the kind of communication that took place between my staff and me, not to mention my clients and me at that time. My concern was not that this was going to be the end of the world. No, not at all. My concern was that *they*—at least some of them—thought this was going to be the end of the world. When you believe something that is untrue, you jump to conclusions, and you make decisions that may not be in your best interests. I didn't want that to happen to our clients. I'm hopeful that we and they continue on the path that has been proven to work for us time after time.

Setbacks will happen. Volatility will happen. Think of it like the weather. One day, you wake up and it's spring. As you engage in all the activities you love, you feel positive, maybe even uplifted. You're feeling so great that you think about renting a cabin in the mountains, maybe even remodeling your kitchen, updating your patio, or putting in a swimming pool.

Then something happens to change that attitude of yours—a rainstorm perhaps, or a triple-digit, blazing hot day. Does that prevent you from ever again going outside? I hope not. The weather on one day does not represent how the weather will always be. It will not affect how you will decide to invest your time and/or money. You know spring will come again, and maybe this rainstorm is the perfect opportunity for you to invest in a summer cabin, a kitchen or patio remodel, or a swimming pool while prices are rock bottom.

NOT TOO BAD, NOT TOO GOOD: SOMEWHERE IN THE MIDDLE

Many think they can sell high and buy low. If you have a really good market, it defies all the conventional wisdom. People have a lack of confidence, so they don't want to stay with it. Speculative cycles will set in, and that's what happened in 2007 and 2008. In the 1990s, many people thought you could continue with a return of 18 percent a year. I knew otherwise, and so did my clients (because I shared that information with them). As I've said before, the attitude for successful investing is not getting excited while you're making money. It's not about the fear that hits you when you realize that you aren't making and might even be losing money. It's about living your life in a positive way and knowing that you've made a solid investment that, down the road, you and your family can count on.

If you have too much confidence, you're no longer cautious, you're no longer fearful, and you buy. It's kind of the reverse of lacking so much confidence that you're afraid to do anything. Here's the cycle. You start out so fearful that you can't do anything, and then you get to the point where you have no fear, and you're totally confident that somehow things will continue as they are. Neither of these emotional states is based in truth. The fallacy that people allow themselves to get trapped into is not knowing the difference. It's thinking that things are either too bad or too good. Instead, you have to try to get in the middle and not allow your emotion to drive your actions.

For example, regardless of what happens to the market, I won't do anything today based on anything I learned today. I won't sell anything based on anything I learned today. That's the outlook you need to work toward, and it's the opposite of what drives most people. It's tempting to want to outsmart others or the market, but you will only harm yourself. Part of the investor's outlook is the ability to shut off the right-now and revert to the logical side of your brain. It's there, and the more you practice staying there, the easier time you'll have maintaining the investor's outlook.

Remember, the greatest compromiser of intelligence is emotion. You can talk yourself into thinking you're acting on data and intelligence. Again, reason tells you one thing and emotion tells you another. Not everyone can discern the voice of reason. If they buy a stock, and it goes up, it's good. If it goes down, they sell it, no matter what their analysis tells them if it doesn't match up in the short run. My rule: you have to trust your analysis; you have to trust your numbers.

Human nature being what it is, I do need to speak with my clients when they react emotionally. I try to draw on history, to point out how many times before we found ourselves in similar circumstances, and those who had the patience to hold on were rewarded. Those who didn't ran into problems.

I recommend that you do the same. Think about everything we've been through in our history—the wars, the depression, and other financial crises. We survived them.

My clients tend to be older, so whatever I'm speaking to them about usually resonates because they've been there before and have probably made the same mistake they're currently contemplating. In such a situation, I am not judgmental because I understand what someone who has put faith in me and in the stock market is dealing with. Being an investor from roughly 2000 to 2010 was really painful. My new clients didn't experience that with me, so they don't have a true understanding of what happened. But my older clients did, and they know I was right at that time. They know that conviction and faith and belief are rewarded, but you sometimes have to live through a lot of pain. That's a lesson that's taught in everything we do.

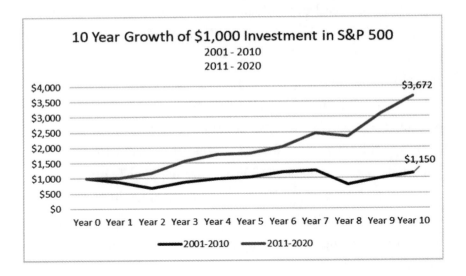

My job is to remind the older clients what happened before and to explain it to the new clients. I try to be calm, and I try to be consistent. People who work with me know that I'm never going to tell them to sell.

CAN IT BE THAT EASY?

In a way, investing is easy if you have the attitude of a long-term investor and not a get-in/get-out one. Here's how my firm approaches it. First, if I'm looking over all the publications I read, I can promise you that I will not buy or sell based on anything I learned today. I am 100 percent confident that if I buy companies that meet my qualifications, I will reap that 10 percent over time. So how do I do that? How do I make those decisions? Here's a simple way of looking at it.

Companies in which I invest must meet the following qualifications:

- They are well managed.

- They are free of much debt.

- They have a solid history of growth.

There are no exceptions. Most people want to look at everything. Their mantra is, "Maybe this time it's different."

"Maybe it is," I agree, but I'm not going to waste my time looking at it. I'd rather get a bunch of gems around me. I have always managed and invested by rules, and I think too many manage by exception. Everything that comes across is subject to negotiation. I learned in my earliest years that if you do that in a business, you create a culture of deals and suspicion that somebody is getting something that one or another is not getting. You create confusion. When you invest by exception, you do the same thing; you confuse a situation that might have been clear-cut before. For example, I will not buy a company without a return on equity of at least 10 percent.

That's it. If that sounds too easy, know that it would be if we didn't often have the human elements of doubt and greed getting in the way.

My son Kevin and I sometimes speak to various financial groups, people who are in our business, where we give a PowerPoint presentation. Yes, I know that many say it's "no power and no point," but I think we make our presentations relevant. When we started speaking to these groups, they would look at our history and our record, and by their expressions and their questions, I could tell they were impressed.

Then the questions started coming.

"How many analysts do you have?"

"How much coverage do you have?"

"Where do you do this?"

"Where do you have that?"

That's when I realized that we were making it look too easy by boiling everything we do down to the basics. But here's the truth. The numbers *are* basic, and so is investing if you have the right mindset and the investor's outlook. The human element is much more complicated. You can make it look complicated to impress someone, but you won't gain anything by doing that. One of my goals for this book is to show you how simple it can be so that when you hear a pitch that's too good to be true, or when you try to talk yourself into an unwise move, you can go back to the basics and know it's OK to just do nothing for a moment.

There are people out there who will boast that they're great because they have more analysts or they do more deals. Well, if that's the criteria you're measuring excellence on, all right—I guess you're great. But the measure of excellence should be getting the job done, the numbers, the results. Unlike most industries, we are in a quantifiable business, and that's fortunate for us because we have a track record to rival those who are trying to make the business more complicated than it needs to be.

THE SALAD OIL SCANDAL

An example of simplicity is an American Express scandal that took place in the early 1960s. Warren Buffett made a lot of money in a short period of time because he purchased a 5 percent stake in American Express around the time of what became known as the salad oil scandal.

One of the worst scams of the era, this took place when New Jersey Allied Crude Vegetable Oil Company executives found out that banks would make loans secured by the company's soybean (salad) oil inventory. Someone came up with the bright idea of floating the oil on water so that when the holding tanks were tested, inspectors would be fooled into thinking the whole tank was full of oil. Anthony De Angelis, a commodities trader and Allied founder, was behind the scam (and later served prison time for it). He hoped to corner the soybean oil market, drive up the price, and raise the value for both his future and underlying commodity positions. Among the largest providers of loans to Allied was American Express. To get more loans, Allied began falsifying loans, claiming far more soybean oil than even in those tampered storage tanks.[28]

Enter a whistleblower in 1963, and the truth came to light that $175 million worth of salad oil didn't exist. The market responded accordingly. American Express was stuck holding the bill on the bad loans and dealing with a significant decrease in its market value. During the fallout, Buffett purchased his 5 percent stake, and it was one of his early successes. When asked to see his file for American Express, he gave the auditors a little file with a couple of pieces of paper in it. The situation might have sounded complicated, but his explanation of purchasing the shares was simple.

If you go to many large firms, they will bury you in data. I think it gets in the way. What do you need to know? This is what you need to do. Do it. If you don't understand what I'm saying, name one great business leader who professes to be a lawyer by training. Simplicity is underrated, but it's the best approach. Otherwise you'll have paralysis by analysis, and there's a lot of that in our world today.

> **Simplicity is underrated, but it's the best approach. Otherwise you'll have paralysis by analysis, and there's a lot of that in our world today.**

---

28 James Chen, "Salad Oil Scandal," Investopedia, July 25, 2015, https://www.investopedia.com/terms/s/saladoilscandal.asp.

Too often when listening to others in my profession, I find myself thinking, *Why are you making it so difficult? It doesn't have to be.* One of my goals with this book is to show you that it doesn't have to be complicated and that when you are able to control the way you think about investing and honor the way you feel about investing—and when you make the commitment—everything else will pretty much fall into place. It won't happen overnight, but it won't require years of study or speaking a language few understand either.

When I talk about simplicity, I like to quote Peter Lynch, who managed the Magellan Fund for Fidelity. "Go for a business that any idiot can run—because sooner or later any idiot probably is going to be running it."

COMPOUNDING

Compounding is what happens when you invest for the long term. It's the way your money grows, in spurts but with certainty. And while your investment grows, so does the amount it grows by. Think of what happens with credit card debt if you pay only the minimum payment. You end up handing large chunks of money to the credit card company. Compounding returns in your investments is the opposite of paying debt on a credit card. You are handing the chunks to yourself—for later.

Simple interest is just that. If you have $1,000 in an account that pays you 3 percent simple interest annually, you'll collect $30 each year. If the interest is compounded, then you will get $30 in your first year, and if you have $1,030 in your account the next year, you'll collect 3 percent of that, or $30.90.

After thirty years, that thirty dollars you might have decided to spend on dinner before you made the decision to invest it would grow to $7,064, and in forty years, it would grow to $72,132. And that magic happens at a rate of only 3 percent?

So why doesn't everybody do that? Because they don't have the investor's outlook, and because they aren't getting the right information.

RULES FOR DEVELOPING THE INVESTOR'S OUTLOOK

Your outlook will develop after you learn and practice some of my rules.

PATIENCE

We've already discussed that nothing happens overnight and that when you control your emotions, you control your outcomes.

Paul A. Samuelson, the first American Nobel laureate in economics and the foremost academic economist of the twentieth century, said, "Investing should be more like watching paint dry or watching grass grow. If you want excitement, take eight hundred dollars and go to Las Vegas."

In other words, know the difference between investing and gambling.

NOT ASSUMING YOU CAN SOMEHOW SELL HIGH AND BUY LOW

As I explained earlier in this chapter, people who think they can do that wind up buying high and selling low, just the reverse of their intentions.

HONESTY ABOUT YOUR TOLERANCE FOR VOLATILITY: LESS IS FREQUENTLY MORE

Suppose we start out, and I determine from what someone is saying—and the emotions behind their words—that having half of their money in the stock market is the maximum for them. Usually it's not uncommon for them to either say, "No, it should be less," or "It should be more." Again, it's up to them and how comfortable they are with risk.

I often tell them, "Less is more for you," and at first they don't understand what I mean by that.

My point is that if I push someone so much into stocks that it makes them uncomfortable to the point that they cannot hold, they will succumb to emotion, and we don't want to go there. Remember, the benefit is long term, and if you feel uncertain, be honest about it.

I'd rather tell that person I described to start with 20 percent or 30 percent in stocks rather than 70 percent or 80 percent because if I can keep them in the market, they will do far better than if they had 80 percent in stocks while buying and selling and getting frightened out and then buying again.

I've found that approach to be better for me and better for the client and better for everybody. I'll confess that when I was younger and still had all the answers, I was looking for the optimum for my clients and for me. What I've learned over the years and do my best to practice is that the optimum for everyone is different. For me, it's all the way with stocks.

If I were exiting when the market is bad, I'd be speaking out of both sides of my mouth, but I'm going to be there regardless of what happens. Yes, it's tough when things don't work out the way I want them to, but jumping off a bridge isn't an option, and you just deal with it. You tell yourself—because it's the truth—that a better day is coming.

That's what I do, but I know I'm comfortable with volatility because I've lived with it most of my life and because it's paid off for me. When it comes to my clients—and to you—it's a personal decision, and there is no wrong answer as long as you're honest with yourself.

You want your investing journey to be constant. Yes, stocks will grow in spurts, but if you react that way, you won't be able to tolerate the experience for long. The good news is that everyone does not have to invest the same way or take on the same amount of risk.

WHAT YOU MUST REMEMBER ABOUT INVESTING

- Growth comes in spurts.

- Never personalize market volatility leading to temporary losses.

- The attitude for successful investing is not getting excited while you're making money or getting afraid when you realize that you aren't making and might even be losing money.

- Companies in which I invest must be well managed, free of much debt, and have a solid history of growth.

- Investing (and investment advice) doesn't have to be complicated, but it must be sound.

- Compounding is a sure way to build wealth.

So where do you get the right investment information? The next chapter will help you evaluate.

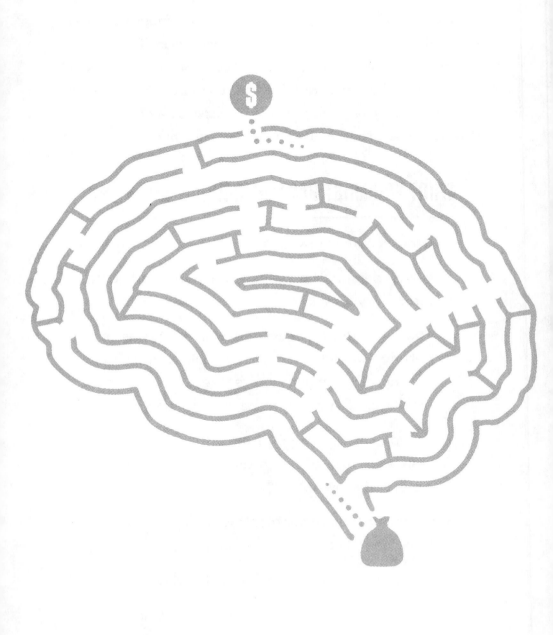

CHAPTER SIX

WHERE DO YOU GET YOUR FINANCIAL ADVICE?

Curranism #6: *"Don't be one of those people who wants bad advice. Many do, and much of it is out there."*

You turn on the television, and an "expert" tells you how you ought to be investing your money—something you're not doing and have never done. Instead of wondering about the expert's qualifications or changing channels, you start to worry. Or you check out investing news on your phone and decide you need to go with a hot stock. *Why didn't your investment professional tell you about this?* you wonder.

Someone advises you—as I already have in this book—that your house should not be the place to put most of your investment dollars. But now you just heard how someone has made a fortune investing in homes. Where are you supposed to turn, and what are you supposed to believe?

Although following the media might be a good way to detect when bull or bear markets are evolving, media reports can also be outdated, short lived, or even nonsensical and based on rumors. Ultimately, individual investors are accountable for their own trade decisions and must be cautious when seeking to time market opportunities based on the latest headlines. Using rational and realistic thinking to understand when an investment may be in a development cycle is the key to evaluating interesting opportunities and resisting bad investing ideas. Reacting to the latest breaking news is probably a sign that decisions are being driven by emotion rather than rational thinking.[29]

Many people pick up their beliefs, confusion, and anxiety from what they hear their peers say, by what they see online, and by what financial media tells them. Yes, too many people get their investment advice from the television.

Now that you know you've got to make long-term investments in stocks, you have to determine where you're going to get your information. Please let it be from experts.

If you visit our offices, you'll never see us playing CNBC or the Fox Business channel. That's because we don't trust finance celebrities, and neither should you.

NO ACCOUNTABILITY

It goes back to the problem of investment salespeople. Finance celebrities are in the business of promoting, not the business of making you

---

29 Kristina Zucchi, "How to Avoid Emotional Investing," Investopedia, Feb. 2, 2020, https://www.investopedia.com/articles/basics/10/how-to-avoid-emotional-investing.asp.

build wealth. Because they are working in the world of short-term investing, nobody ever looks back a month or a year later to see how their advice fared. They offer no data, and they aren't held to any kind of standard. Investors like Warren Buffett don't try to predict the market, but people on your TV screen do.

If people get paid for talking, they talk. It doesn't mean all the advice they offer is bad or that they're purposely trying to lead you astray. Their goal is to get you to listen; it's what they get paid for.

HOW DO YOU KNOW THEY'RE ANY GOOD?

If you profess to be good at something, there should be some metric that shows how good you are. Is it knowledge in your field, or is it the ability to ring the cash register? We have no filters when we turn on the TV. The fact that someone is there is instant credibility. I had an acquaintance that rose at 4 a.m. to be on TV. He made a career out of that. And it, not his knowledge of investing, was what rang his cash register.

This is even more worrisome when you consider how few people are interested in investment advice. Pre-COVID, in 2019, a survey found that 75 percent of Americans managed their own finances—despite the fact that not even half of all adults could cover an unexpected $1,000 expense. Only 17 percent said they used a financial advisor.[30] If people are not working with a financial advisor, where are they getting their information?

---

30 Jessica Dickler, "75% of Americans are Winging It When It Comes to Their Financial Future," CNBC, April 2, 2019, https://www.cnbc.com/2019/04/01/when-it-comes-to-their-financial-future-most-americans-are-winging-it.html.

INSTANT NEWS

Please get your news anywhere other than social media. The instant news is available every hour of every day, and it is the equivalent of tabloid news. Someone in a position like mine can't outshout it, so we need to correct the so-called facts they spread.

For many users, social media is part of their daily routine. Roughly three-quarters of Facebook users and around six in ten Instagram users visit these sites at least once a day.

When BBC Future Now interviewed a panel of fifty experts in early 2017 about the "grand challenges we face in the twenty-first century," many named the breakdown of trusted information sources.

"The major new challenge in reporting news is the new shape of truth," said Kevin Kelly, cofounder of *Wired* magazine. "Truth is no longer dictated by authorities but is networked by peers. For every fact there is a counterfact, and all these counterfacts and facts look identical online, which is confusing to most people."[31]

A Pew Research Center analysis of surveys conducted between October 2019 and June 2020 found that those who rely most on social media for political news differed from other news consumers in a number of ways. These US adults tend to be less likely than other news consumers to closely follow major news stories, such as the coronavirus outbreak and the 2020 presidential election. Perhaps tied to that, this group also tends to be less knowledgeable about these topics.[32]

---

31 Janna Anderson and Lee Rainie. "The Future of Truth and Misinformation Online," Pew Research Center, Oct. 19, 2017, https://www.pewresearch.org/internet/2017/10/19/the-future-of-truth-and-misinformation-online/.

32 Amy Mitchell, Mark Jurkowitz, J. Baxter Oliphant, and Elisa Shearer, "Americans Who Mainly Get Their News on Social Media Are Less Engaged, Less Knowledgeable," Pew Research Center, July 30, 2020, https://www.pewresearch.org/journalism/2020/07/30/americans-who-mainly-get-their-news-on-social-media-are-less-engaged-less-knowledgeable/.

However, another study found that investors are, in fact, influenced by comments attached to financial disclosures they see on social media. In keeping with prior research on herding and social media, investors are also influenced by majority opinions delivered by way of social media comments. When investors received all positive comments attached to both good and bad news, their perception of the news was significantly more positive than when the comments were all negative and when no comments were attached. The effect is most noteworthy in the case where bad news is disclosed and all positive comments were attached to the post. In this case, the bad news was perceived as good news.[33]

THE HUMAN APPROACH

When you're investing, you're not a paint-by-number person; you are still yourself with your personality and your tolerance for volatility. You may not be aware of that until you work one-on-one with someone. As I was writing this book, my firm opened a new client account with a forty-year-old man who had won a settlement for several millions. Prior to that, he had no investments and some savings, so of course he was apprehensive. As we spoke, I could sense his fear, and I knew he would not be comfortable in the investments that would ultimately earn the most for him. It's not about how I'll be comfortable investing; it's only about how you will.

I really try to understand not what someone says but who they are, because once we're into the relationship, I know I can build their

---

33   Brad S. Trinkle, Robert E. Crossler, and F. Bélanger, "Voluntary Disclosures via Social Media and the Role of Comments," Semantic Scholar, 2015, https://www.semanticscholar.org/paper/Voluntary-Disclosures-via-Social-Media-and-the-Role-Trinkle-Crossler/8455f650d29a611ac5a49e18b84dc82 2ad2c4897.

confidence. None of this happens if the investor is just collecting information online and trying to make decisions based on that.

Remember, instant news is not news. The fact that some people trust it is disturbing. I feel that people in my position with long-term clients who trust us have earned that trust. We deal with numbers, with hard facts, and we do our best to remain consistent. The sources of instant news haven't earned your trust or your loyalty, and they are frequently inconsistent.

I'm not saying don't go to the websites, read the publications, or occasionally listen to someone's opinion on television. You don't have to cover your eyes when they pop up—which they do—just about everywhere. Just be aware that they would not be there if they weren't benefitting.

In addition to the regular talking heads, finance networks feature experts as guests. These people appear for no pay to share their opinions. Some are politicians, some are journalists, and some are stock analysts. Each has a reason and a potential personal benefit for being there.

The next time you see a talking head speaking about the market, ask yourself what's in it for them.

WHY YOU MIGHT AS WELL CHANGE THE CHANNEL

- Too many people make or put off investment decisions based on what they see on TV.

- Finance celebrities are in the business of promoting.

- Be aware of what's in it for them.

- Seek advice from experts.

I've spent a lot of time talking to you about how important it is to invest. Now I want to share what the future holds if you don't.

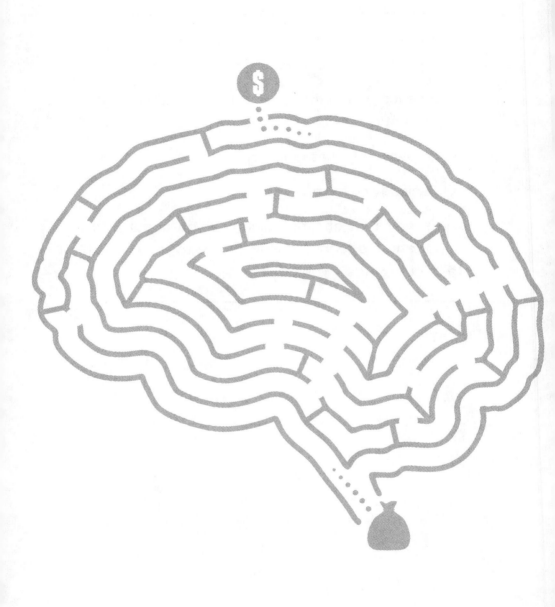

CHAPTER SEVEN

LOOKING AT A DOLLAR IN FUTURE TERMS

Curranism #7: *"Future retirement income cannot be paid for in current dollars. The future always costs more."*

In addition to helping my clients provide for their futures, I try to help them better understand challenges we all face with life expectancies that are extending our time on this earth into our nineties and perhaps longer.

The message for them and for you is this: depend on yourself, and no one else, to pay for your retirement. If you are older, you have the luck to have been born earlier. Social Security can still pay benefits to older persons based on rather slim contributions you made in your early years of working. You may even be fortunate enough to receive a defined benefit (pension) check each month along with Social Security.

If you are younger, pay particular attention to my experience compared to what you face now and will face as you approach retirement. Slim contributions paid to Social Security by me and earlier generations have become significantly larger as a percentage of your earnings.

Governments have done a poor job understanding what it means for Social Security benefits when people live longer while having fewer children. Compounding the problem is the tendency to expand benefits without fully understanding future increased costs. More people are promised benefits and fewer workers to pay, so the challenge to sustain programs for retirees has become overwhelming.

When I began working after college, I earned about $8,000. My wife, Peg, earned about $7,000. I was a recent graduate of the University of Pennsylvania's Wharton School, having earned an MBA. Peg graduated from Temple University with a BS in Education. The year was 1969. I was working in Albany, New York, as a business improvement analyst in the New York State Department of Transportation. Peg taught fourth grade in the Bethlehem Central School District.

Keep in mind we had both recently graduated from college. We were on track to receive the maximum Social Security benefit at our full retirement age of sixty-six. We did not know it at the time, but that would have been $2,366 per month. If delayed until age seventy, the benefit would have been about $3,123 per month.

So in our very first year of full-time employment, we were on track to receive a maximum Social Security benefit at our full retirement age of sixty-six.

To actually receive the full retirement benefit would require at least thirty-five years of earnings in excess of the amount subject to

Social Security tax. By 2011 (my full retirement age), the maximum taxable earnings subject to Social Security tax had risen to $106,800, and the rate was 5.7 percent plus Medicare of 1.45 percent.

Those beginning their working lives in 2020 would need to earn $137,000 in their first year of employment to qualify for the maximum Social Security benefit at their full retirement age of sixty-seven. I needed earnings of $7,000 to qualify for a maximum benefit. Keep in mind that to qualify for a maximum benefit, the worker must reach the threshold for earnings in thirty-five of their working years. I do not know many young workers whose careers promise a starting salary of $137,700. In 1969, when my wife and I began our careers, we reached maximum Social Security earnings at the entry level for New York Civil Service employees and as a first-year teacher.

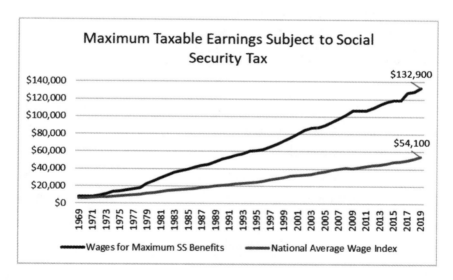

The Medicare portion is on all earnings. There is no cap. As of January 2013, individuals with earned income of more than $200,000 ($250,000 for married couples filing jointly) pay an additional 0.9 percent in Medicare taxes. The previous amount does not include the

0.9 percent Medicare tax. Beginning in 1984, Medicare was charged on all earnings without a cap.

In 1969, the maximum I could have paid in Social Security taxes was $395.50. My employer would have paid the same for my account. Today, the maximum paid would be $10,534 by the employee with the employer paying an equal amount.

I am a financial person with a financial mind. So when I consider the costs relative to the benefits, I conclude all of us better make sure we focus on our personal financial security. It becomes increasingly difficult for younger people because they are being asked to assume a much larger financial burden than their parents and grandparents.

Those dollars are being spent today to pay for benefits to currently retired and disabled people. They are taxed to younger working people who do so with the promise they will receive future benefits.

When we look at the present value of the tax for someone who earns $137,000, the numbers are simple enough to understand. The employee pays $10,534, and the employer pays the same. The total is $21,068.

Let's also consider what happens when two people filing joint tax returns each earn $68,850. Their tax paid as a family would be the same as if only one worked and earned $137,700.

When I consider a dollar, I always look at it in future terms. As I have written so many times in the past, the long-term growth in stocks has been about 10 percent. From the time I began full-time employment in 1969 to my full retirement in 2011, stocks appreciated 9.85 percent annually.

What do you suppose the future value of $8,537 could be if a couple in 2020 had combined earnings of $137,000 and invested $8,537 in the stock market represented by the S&P 500? Do not forget the combined tax they pay to include Medicare is $10,524, and their employer is paying the same for their benefit. The sum is $21,148 when all is included. We are considering only $8,537 or 40 percent.

Let's say they are twenty-eight years old and plan to quit working at their current full retirement age of sixty-seven as defined by Social Security.

What do you suppose the future value is for $8,537 in thirty-nine years invested with a possible return of 10 percent? Keep in mind the worst thirty-five-year rolling period for the S&P 500 was 1930–1964. The annualized return was 9.4 percent. Longer time periods have higher returns that average about 10 percent.

$8,537 would grow to $351,253 at our couple's year for full retirement in thirty-nine years. $351,253 is the equivalent of 116 payments of $3,011 (maximum monthly benefit in 2020). Those 116 payments are almost ten full years of benefits at the 2020 maximum. It still leaves thirty-eight additional payments to grow.

Of course, the future value doubles if the employer contribution is included. But what is truly astonishing is when all thirty-nine years are included and the future value becomes $3,778,412. When we include the employer contribution, the future value is $7,556,824. Do not forget the trend for Social Security contributions has been steady increases. In our illustration we show the same Social Security contribution over the entire thirty-nine years.

When I began full time employment in 1969 the tax was $374 for the employee. When the employer portion is included, it was $748. In 2020 the amounts were $8,537 and $17,074! The increase was about twenty-three times greater than when I began working in 1969.

Here's my point. Spending without investment is a road to financial ruin. When you don't responsibly invest to secure your financial security, the outcome is not good. When the government requires so much to fund Social Security, it takes away dollars you could invest for your own retirement, making the problem worse.

When the government requires so much to fund Social Security, it takes away dollars you could invest for your own retirement, making the problem worse.

You can spend a dollar only one time. In this case, many dollars are being taxed to provide a benefit in retirement that is promoted *not* to be to be relied upon as the sole source for your retirement income.

The amounts being paid for Social Security could fund retirements much more efficiently, requiring far less expense to do so.

If you do not agree, consider this fact. Social Security is 27 percent of the federal budget.

Let's forget postcollege earnings for now. I worked in high school and during my college years. Here are my earnings during my school years:

- 1960: $155 (high school freshman)

- 1961: $445

- 1962: $235

- 1963: $1,890 (graduated from high school in June)

- 1964: $1,930 (college freshman in September)

- 1965: $1,962

- 1966: $2,453

- 1967: $1,415 (graduated from college and married)

- 1968: $2,991 (graduate student)

The total of my school year contributions for Social Security were $496. Not included were Medicare taxes, known as hospital insurance, which began in 1966. Initially they were 0.7 percent, and by the time I became a full-time employee in 1969, they were 1.2 percent.

Social Security taxes in 1960 were 6 percent (3 percent paid by employee and 3 percent paid by the employer). By 2020 the combined tax rate had risen to 15.3 percent. It is shared equally by the employee and employer, with each paying 7.65 percent. The cap on income has risen to $137,700. The Medicare portion is 1.45 percent and has no income cap. It is also shared equally by the employee and employer. However, individuals with income greater than $200,000 and couples with more than $250,000 pay an additional 0.9 percent with no salary cap.

I am always saying you can spend a dollar only once. It is also true that you can only invest a dollar one time, but when the money is spent presumably for your benefit, it cannot be invested.

So back when I was working part time in high school and college, $496 I paid in Social Security taxes plus the $496 paid by my employers were used to pay benefits to eligible people in 1960–1969.

The same dollars invested in the S&P 500 would have grown to $54,959 by my full retirement age in 2012. It is a sum equal to about a full two years of benefits paid to me.

Let's look at what someone today is paying at current rates and salary caps.

When costs are discussed with regard to Social Security as I have, inevitably the discussion shifts to defending Social Security or suggesting reform. I am doing neither but would prefer to concentrate on how I measure cost as it relates to your retirement security.

Most people measure everything in present value terms. For example, how much is the price of a coffee? How much is the cost of a car or house?

Before we go further, let me explain. In 1969, I paid the maximum into Social Security. The maximum taxable earnings subject to Social Security taxes in 1969 was $7,000. The total I paid was 4.2 percent, or $336. Then, like now, the employer matched and paid the same. Peg paid the same, as did her employer.

Medicare was passed by Congress in 1965 with taxes beginning in 1966. In 1969, the maximum taxable earnings subject to the tax was the same as Social Security, $7,000. Between its inaugural year in 1966 and 1969, it was raised two times in three years. Initially it was set at .7 percent. In 1967, it was 1 percent, and in 1968, 1.2 percent. It is known as hospital insurance tax and is in addition to Social Security. The hospital insurance tax was for each of us. The total paid by Peg and me was $840. Our payroll tax was equal to 5.6 percent of our gross income. If we count the part paid by our employers, it would make it 11.2 percent of our income.

Payroll taxes, like Social Security, are fairly easy to quantify because they are fixed based on income and do not allow for personal choice. For example, a sales tax can be reduced by simply buying a less expensive car or not buying a car. Payroll taxes do not allow for personal choice.

The solutions to each Social Security shortfall in the past have been to do the following:

- Increase the tax rate.

- Increase the upper limit on income subject to Social Security tax.

- Increase the age to reach full retirement.

- Reduce the rate of increase in retiree benefits.

- Change the formula for calculating cost of living adjustments that significantly reduced increases in benefits.

- In 1983, Congress passed laws that made part of Social Security income subject to federal income taxes.

When I first contributed to Social Security, my share of the tax was $395.50. My benefit at the Social Security full retirement age (sixty-six) was $2,366. I received a monthly benefit equal to 7.04 times my annual Social Security tax I paid in 1969.

Let's say a young person who just graduated from college did make the maximum subject to Social Security taxes in 2020. They would pay $10,534. If they were to be paid the same multiple I was at their full retirement age, they would receive $74,159.36 per month! How likely is that?

WHAT YOU NEED TO REMEMBER

- Depend on yourself, and no one else, to pay for your retirement.

- Many dollars are being taxed to provide a benefit in retirement that is promoted *not* to be relied upon as the sole source for your retirement income.

- You can only invest a dollar one time, but when the money is spent presumably for your benefit, it cannot be invested.

- Spending without investment is a road to financial ruin.

- Payroll taxes do not allow for personal choice.

- When it comes to Social Security, those of us who are older are receiving a much better deal than those who are younger.

So where should you turn for guidance on investing? My clients turn to me, and I try to provide them with not just accurate information and wise, well-thought-out advice, but with a sense of stability. These are uncertain times, but then, I've lived seven decades, and I can't recall a time that was not uncertain. As I've said elsewhere, whatever current crisis is happening to us right now feels like the worst one. Recent years certainly have. However, if you have an investor's outlook, you are in it for the long run. At some point, you're going to seek out the help of an advisor. The next chapter will show you how to do that.

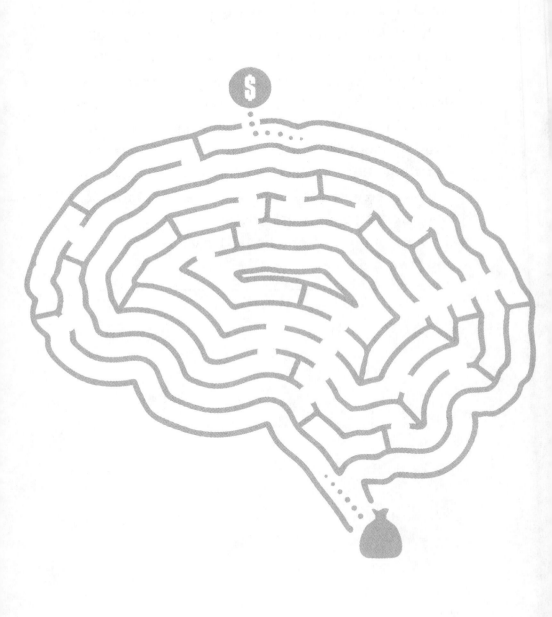

CHAPTER EIGHT

PREPARING FOR YOUR FUTURE, WHATEVER YOUR AGE

Curranism #8: *"If you do it every day,
you can do it in microseconds."*

Do you need an investment advisor? Maybe one of the reasons you picked up this book is that you're not sure about the answer to that question. Obviously, you know what I would say, but what about you? In most cases, I believe your answer should be yes.

WHY DO YOU NEED ONE?

Are you comfortable with your portfolio? Are you comfortable with (or do you even have) an investment advisor? You may be wondering about how much home to buy, how to plan for your children's college, saving for retirement, or planning your estate. At each of these important life stages, you need someone without any emotional skin in the game to help you come up with a path.

Suppose someone leaves you a large sum of money. Do you invest it? In what? How much of it? Maybe you lose your job or want to take early retirement. How much money should you take out of your IRA or retirement fund? These are major questions, and you'll be more confident making a plan with someone who's dealt with similar situations over a long period of time, good economy and bad economy.

WHEN DO YOU NEED ONE?

From the point of view of discipline, you could probably benefit from a very early age. You need that voice of reason saying, "Hey, you don't need a $35,000 car. Take a look at what this money can do for you."

You're never too young for this kind of advice, and you're never too old. The biggest reason people achieve or don't achieve in life is discipline or the lack of it. As I've said throughout this book, financial security is achieved by regular and methodical investing and holding. If you keep giving in to the emotion of buying or the emotion of fear, the yo-yo of saving and spending will keep going down until you're pretty close to rock bottom. More money will not magically appear. The right—and I emphasize the word *right* here—advisor can keep you from succumbing to temptation by doing something that sounds very simple but which, in real life, is a little more complex. And that is tell you the truth.

When you are on a rocky emotional cliff, you need someone who can remind you that you are letting your emotions rule, which will remind you why you need to slow down and take a deep breath. Most professional advisors agree regarding the consequences of emotional investing.

- Investing based on emotion (greed or fear) is the main reason why so many people are buying at market tops and selling at market bottoms.

- Underestimating risks associated with investments is one reason why investors sometimes make suboptimal decisions based on emotion.

- During periods of market volatility, investors often move funds from riskier stocks to lower-risk interest-bearing securities.

- Dollar-cost averaging and diversification are two approaches that investors can implement to make consistent decisions that are not driven by emotion.

- Staying the course through short-term volatility is often the key to longer-term success as an investor.[34]

Your investment advisor can remind you of the need for someone you can trust, not a cheerleader who makes you feel good. More than anything, you need someone who absolutely tells you, in a realistic way, what you must do. You have to have confidence that he or she can help force you to do what you haven't done on your own and what you need to do immediately and in the future based on your circumstances. Furthermore, and very importantly, this person must have a plan and must be able to demonstrate that they've executed the plan so you can have a higher degree of trust that they can do it going forward. Remember, those of us who do this every day and who are deeply invested ourselves

---

34 Zucchi, "How to Avoid Emotional Investing."

live and breathe investing. It's not a hobby, not something you can sit down on the weekend and do with software, however sophisticated.

So much in the investment business is all about bravado and sizzle. I encourage you to avoid both. Instead, choose an advisor the way you'd choose a surgeon. Finding the right person is not about financial acumen alone. It's about trust and demonstrating that the person you put that trust in has done what they're advising you to do.

HOW TO CONNECT

This is not your parents' investment world. Today, you have your choice of dealing through apps and websites, on the phone, or in person.

The term "financial advisor" may describe a financial planner, an online service, or even a firm like mine. Some of the robo-sites can manage a portfolio for you. You'll fill out a questionnaire, and the algorithm will probably suggest a portfolio of index funds and low-cost exchange-traded funds. The next step up in the price range is an online service. Some of these provide virtual meetings between you and an advisor. Some charge a flat fee. Others charge a fee for investment managing and offer additional sessions with an advisor.

Then there are real people who offer real advice to other real people who aren't sure what they should be doing with their momentarily real money. Here are some of the most popular designations.

A Certified Financial Planner (CFP) has completed an education requirement, passed a test, demonstrated work experience, and been designated by the Certified Financial Planner Board of Standards.

A wealth manager provides, as the name suggests, wealth management for clients who typically have a high net worth.

A stockbroker buys and sells financial products, usually on commission, although this has changed in these days when few investors trust advice from those on commission. A stockbroker or broker must pass exams and register with the US Securities and Exchange Commission.

An RIA, registered investment advisor, is registered with the US Securities and Exchange Commission or a state regulator. An RIA is a fee-based advisor who makes recommendations. That's what I am. People pay us a fee to help them. At the end of the day, you've hired me to help you reach your goals. As I said before, a lot of people in the business get commissions directly connected to what you buy. I'd rather be paid not based on what you buy but by the value of my advice.

Most of the big national firms are registered both ways. They can put on both the commission hat and the fee hat.

> **I'd rather be paid not based on what you buy but by the value of my advice.**

I don't think you can do that, but they say they can. I was uncomfortable doing it back in my early days, and I still am.

The industry makes it difficult for us. For instance, most insurance products are commission based. I can't say to a client, "We're going to buy this life insurance policy for you. The commissions are $15,000, but we'll rebate it all and charge you a fee of $1,000 a year." The regulators won't let me do that. There's a lot of pressure now, and I believe that one day in the future, you'll have access to insurance products that, like mutual funds, are commission free. I hope it's sooner rather than later.

DO YOU HAVE ENOUGH MONEY TO RETIRE?

Deep breath here. I saved the most difficult question for last. When I wrote this book, I was aware that a twenty-year-old would have more time to put my practices into effect than, say, a sixty-year-old. On the other hand, I knew the sixty-year-old, with the experience and wisdom that come with age, would probably more readily relate to my message. So this book is for you, regardless of how old you are right now.

When we're young, we are (hopefully) asking ourselves what we need to do to have enough money later in life. When we're older, we're asking ourselves if we indeed have enough money. That depends, like all of life, on a lot of circumstances we can't control. So the younger person's question is, "What do I have to do with my earnings to get ready for retirement?" The postretirement person's question is, "How do I change my lifestyle?"

You might say, "If I knew then what I do now, I would do things differently." But we can't go back and change our early decisions. If you play the game the way everybody else does, you should not expect different results. Although retirement will be different from the day you graduated from college or high school and had your whole future ahead, you still can plan regardless of where you are now.

The main things you control in your retirement years are your expenses. Some people sit on a fully paid house, thinking that at least they don't have a mortgage. That doesn't mean the house is free of expenses, though. They still have to deal with maintenance, heating, cooling, taxes. As an example, if you were to sell a fully paid $500,000 house, it wouldn't be uncommon to remove $20,000 to $40,000 of expenses annually. That's like instant income. Invest that money and assume even a 5 percent return on it, and there's another $3,750 a month, which you could use to rent a maintenance-free residence.

THE RULES HAVE CHANGED

People are living longer. That's good news, right? Typically, with a couple sixty-five years old, the probability of one of them living until their nineties is very high. That's close to thirty years. How do you look at the rest of your life? If you consider your working life between the ages of twenty-five and sixty-five, and you are in that range, your plan of attack is going to be different. However, if you are sixty-five, you still have a long time to prepare for.

When we're twenty-five, we think (and often spend as if) we're going to live forever. Retirement is the same way. If you're not careful, you could procrastinate just as you did for the last forty years. Instead, ask yourself the following. Do you really need two cars? Do you really need a five-bedroom house? Whatever you have, that's all you have for the rest of your life—without a paycheck, without a bonus. This is what you have.

THE TRUTH ABOUT "SAFE" INVESTMENTS

I believe that when we're young, we should err on the side of aggressiveness. When we're older, we should err on the side of more conservative investment, which may involve tying up less of our money in stocks. Many people think if they have their money in safe havens (such as cash and short-term bonds) that will assure them financial security, when in truth that may not be the case at all.

Let's suppose you have $100,000 at the first of the year. Inflation is 3 percent over the course of the year, so your purchasing power is down, which leaves you with $97,000. Now, if you earned 2 percent on your investment, and a lot of people do, that means you haven't offset the inflation. Now, let's suppose you take out 4 percent to live. Right away you've spent $4,000, and you're down to less than $96,000. Next year, thanks to inflation, your dollars are worth less, so you will need to withdraw 4.3 percent. That gets you down to less than $90,000 in just two years. You aren't broke, but you are on your way to rock bottom. It's not something you notice right away. You might make subtle adjustments to your lifestyle. Maybe you'll stop going out to dinner or entertaining as often as before. These changes mask the fact—for a while—that your safe investments are anything but.

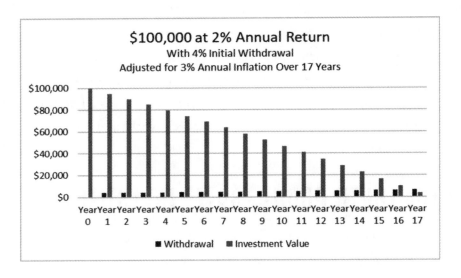

THE CURRAN QUESTIONNAIRE

The previous questions are similar to what I would ask you if we were sitting down, whatever your age, and deciding if we should work together. What sort of future do you envision for yourself? What resources do you have right now to accomplish that? Most people have a vision, and it's easier to talk about visions than absolutes. When I work with clients, I try to take visions and resources and connect them. To achieve your vision, you have to either reduce the vision or increase the resources. If you say, "I want my life to be the way it is now," you can take what you have and what you earn and come to a point of realism.

So ask yourself, "How do I see my retirement?" If your answer is, "I see myself in Florida in the winter, coming back home to visit the family," that life is probably going to take as much money as you're spending in your working years. I've never had someone say, "I'm going to downsize. I'm going to get rid of my Mercedes and buy a Ford." Most visualize a life in retirement like the one they're living. Even if you're nearing retirement age right now, ask yourself what it will take to support that over a thirty-year period. Thirty years is a long time to live without a paycheck.

Ultimately, I look for only one quality in a client, and I would be pleased—and I believe your future would be much improved, not to mention more peaceful and financially secure—if you look for and develop this quality in yourself. That is the quality of believing that steadily and with discipline, you can achieve your financial goals.

You have to be absolutely honest with yourself here because you know you better than anyone else does, so let's evaluate you right now.

Do you have the conviction required in the long term?

Can you carry out a program with discipline, regardless of temptations and fears?

If you have that conviction and that discipline in total or in part, you can be a successful investor. If you don't, if you're going to jump around and live in a state of reaction, you probably lack the outlook and the personality, in my opinion, to be successful with a large (or perhaps any) percentage in the stock market.

> **If you have that conviction and that discipline in total or in part, you can be a successful investor.**

I think by now you can see that I believe outlook is as important as money when it comes to long-term financial success. That's why I don't care how much money a potential client has. I'll choose to work with someone who has $100,000 and a sense of commitment any day over someone with $1 million who does not.

When President Franklin D. Roosevelt gave his first inaugural address, the Great Depression was at its worst. Here's what he said: "This is preeminently the time to speak the truth, the whole truth, frankly and boldly. Nor need we shrink from honestly facing conditions in our country today. This great Nation will endure as it has endured, will revive, and will prosper. So, first of all, let me assert my firm belief that the only thing we have to fear is fear itself—nameless, unreasoning, unjustified terror which paralyzes needed efforts to convert retreat into advance."[35]

- As I was writing, the stock market fell more than 34 percent because of concern over the coronavirus. In 2008, it fell 55 percent. When these things happen, you need to remember, almost as a knee-jerk reaction, that this is not a permanent state; it's short term. It will be resolved, and we will get that average 10 percent long-term return. We will get through it. Furthermore, the recoveries happen very quickly relative to the declines.

- If you sell and come back every time the market bounces up, you will hinder your efforts. As I say earlier in this book, if you have the investor's outlook, you already know what you're going to do when something negative happens. You're not going to be surprised, and you'll know how to talk yourself through it. People who aren't convinced that all the bad things are temporary are in for a tough life. Negative changes *are*

---

35 Franklin D. Roosevelt, Inaugural Address, March 4, 1933, as published in Samuel Rosenman, ed., *The Public Papers of Franklin D. Roosevelt, Volume Two: The Year of Crisis, 1933* (New York: Random House, 1938), 11–16.

temporary; history has proven that time and again.

YOUR TAKEAWAY

- Understand that, regardless of your age, you need a plan for the future.

- Know that steadily and with discipline, you can achieve your financial goals.

- Remember that outlook and your approach are as important as money.

- Don't let fear paralyze you.

As Roosevelt understood all those years ago, fear will paralyze you; it will freeze you and crowd rational thought from your mind. Planning ahead and committing yourself to your plan will give you the power you must have to survive with your financial future secure. I believe that. I would stake all I own on it. Indeed, I have.

This is what I wish for you: commitment, discipline, and most of all the knowledge that if you stick to your plan, regardless of external circumstances, you will achieve and perhaps even surpass your goals.

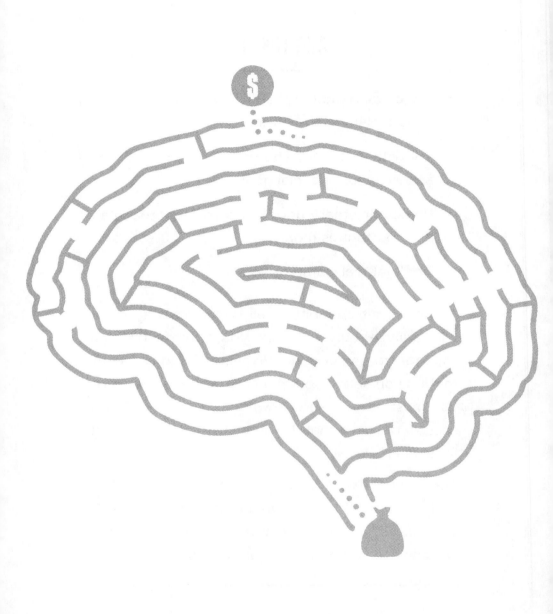

THE CURRANISMS

- When you have too much confidence, you *buy* anything. When you have too much fear, you *don't do* anything. The truth is somewhere in the middle. If things are either too bad or too good, you have to get in the middle.

- Don't underestimate yourself. Don't overestimate others.

- Opportunity knocks all the time. The problem is we just don't hear.

- The term "house poor" exists for a reason.

- Committed long-term investors know that growth in stocks is like adolescent growth spurts. You know they are coming, but you cannot pinpoint the actual timing.

- Don't be one of those people who wants bad advice. Many do, and much of it is out there.

- Future retirement income cannot be paid for in current dollars. The future always costs more.

- If you do it every day, you can do it in microseconds.